My Life On Earth With The Angels

Gwen Charletta McAuley

'Angel Blessings'
Kikis

Gwen McAuley

Copyright © 2012 Gwen McAuley

All rights reserved.

DEDICATION

To the memory of my dear husband, Francis, and my beloved son, Kevin, who inspired me to tell my life story.

ACKNOWLEDGEMENTS

This book would not have been possible without the encouragement of my family and many friends. My sincerest and heartfelt thanks to my sons for encouraging me to tell my life story. They have supported me at every step. Also, to my wide circle of friends, who have always encouraged me to share my story of my Spiritual journey with God and the Angels It is hoped that this book will enlighten others on their own Spiritual journeys, and help those who are having similar experiences to enjoy these loving encounters.

I would also like to express my gratitude to Angela Donnelly, Breige McWilliams Caoimhe Hegarty, Patsy McElwee, Karen McGuigan, Maria McKenna, Christine Chivers, Gavin McGovern and Grainne Keogh-Kelly for all their help.

Photography by Philip McAuley.

Illustration of an Angel drawn by Gavin McGovern.

Illustration of the triangle of bodies by Paula McElwee.

Front cover by Philip McAuley.

CONTENTS:

	Acknowledgements	i
1	AS THE SUN SETS	1
2	THE BEGINNING	4
3	EARLY ENCOUNTERS	6
4	RAY OF LIGHT	13
5	HOME AT LAST	32
6	LIFE'S GREATEST BLESSINGS	42
7	SIGNS FROM THE ANGELS	51
8	MEDJUGORJE	70
9	FAITH AND HOPE IN ILLNESS	81
10	A VEIL OF DARKNESS	90
11	A NEW DAWN	99
12	BEREAVEMENT	104
13	STORIES OF HOPE	113
14	ANGEL MEDITATIONS (1)	134
15	THE TRIANGLE OF LIFE	144
16	ANGEL MEDITATIONS (2)	146
17	ARCHANGEL MICHAEL'S CLEARING EXCERISE	160

Godly Power In Our Universe

*The power of the winds know no boundaries,
without fear they rage on.
The power of the rain keeps falling without fear.
The power of the mountain has no fear, standing
against all the elements.
The power of the universe's growth, it has no fear;
plants, trees and grass keep growing.
The power of the sea keeps ebbing and flowing, it
has no fear.
The power of the sun keeps shining, giving
warmth and light, it has no fear.
Rivers flow on, they have no fear.
The power of the moon and the stars keep beaming
without fear.
Mankind, the highest intelligence in the universe,
because of his fears, worries and concerns, has the
least Godly power of all.*

Gwen McAuley

1
AS THE SUN SETS

Now, in my autumn years, as I look back on my life, I realise that all of my past experiences have been stepping stones on the journey to me reaching my present destination, where I endeavour to live, more out of my soul energy, rather than my physical body. I call this living in the fifth dimension.

My life has been a long, difficult road with many setbacks, as indeed it has been for many others. Today, as I gaze out at the sun setting on the wondrous Sperrin Mountains, I am thankful for everything. I know that if it had not been for certain challenges and many wonderful experiences, my walk with God and the Angels would not have brought me to the place where I am today - a place of peace, love, gratitude, tranquility and contentment.

I suppose I could say that the sun is beginning to set on my walk with God. I have faced trials and suffering, but with God's grace and guidance, I have managed to struggle through and they are now behind me.

My many experiences as an ordinary person have taken me to this place where I have been for such a long time. No one needs any qualifications to reach this peak of spirituality. To live out of our soul's energy just takes time, discipline and perseverance.

My interpretation of life is that we are all born into the fifth dimension. We are born happy, joyful babies. However, we must grow up and we must go to school and learn. Indeed, at this point we slip into the fourth dimension which is a very comfortable place to live.

In the third dimension, just one dimension above the animal kingdom, is the rat race. Many of us lose sight of our true calling. As we grow older, we realise that living in the rat race is not fulfilling our needs; instead, it leaves us feeling empty and sometimes sad and disillusioned. When this happens many people go in search of themselves, trying out many different tactics. I, myself, tried self-awareness and after some time I found this spiritually uplifting and motivating.

When we start to analyse and delve into our self awareness it can be a wake-up call. Perhaps my wake-up call came in 1989 when circumstances in our home were changed forever. It was to be the start of a long and painful journey, not only for me, but for my husband and family. However, out of this pain, I rediscovered myself. I didn't like the new journey I was embarking upon, but with the help of God and the Angels I managed to keep going.

Throughout my journey I have tried many

different forms of prayer. As a young girl, I rhymed off my prayers each morning when I awoke and each night before climbing into bed. As I got older and wiser I turned to God in times of need; when I was worried or anxious, he was always there.

As my faith matured, life for me changed. I not only turned to God in bad times but also in good times. After all, I have had so many blessings in my life: my loving husband, our beautiful sons and my health. Eventually, my faith led me into the prayer of the quiet, otherwise known as meditation.

2
THE BEGINNING

In the depths of winter, as the Second World War raged on, life for many was challenging. Men were being sent off to fight for their country, some never to be seen again, whilst their women were left behind to look after the land and the family. Amid food rations and air raid warning sirens, on the 30th December 1942, the bleakest and coldest of days, Gwendoline Charletta Wolfe, was born. No one could have known that this child's path ahead was to be fraught with so many obstacles. For the first six months of this innocent baby's life, it was as any other young infant's would be. She was loved, nurtured and cared for by her adoring mother and brothers. Her father was not present for the birth as he was posted in France, fighting in the war. But, sadly for little Gwendoline and her siblings, life was to change forever.

On June 22 1943, their mother Charlotte took a cerebral brain haemorrhage and died. News of his young wife's passing reached her husband while in the trenches, but he was injured and unable to make it home for the funeral.

In the weeks following Gwen's mother's death,

a kind neighbour lady took the little baby in. She cared for Gwen for some weeks, but then she, too, died following a tragic road accident. There was no other option but to leave the baby in the care of the state. Little Gwendoline was sent to a wartime orphanage in Belfast. However, this bleak, sad and lonely institution would be the place where Gwen would have her first encounter with the Angels.

3
EARLY ENCOUNTERS

It's difficult to say exactly when I became aware that I seemed to be different from most other people. Possibly, it happened in or around the age of seven. Before I realised that I was different, I took for granted the experiences which I was having with the supernatural (Angels and Jesus etc.). I suppose I just assumed that these were everyday, routine events for everyone. It was only when I was a little older I realised that these experiences were not the norm in our society, in fact, they were something of a taboo subject. Terrified of what people would think of me or say about me, I went all out to conceal them. Like any other young girl I was desperate to fit in with my peers. The last thing I wanted was for them to think that I was strange or odd, so, for most of my early life I kept my gift a closely guarded secret.

However, I have now reached a stage in my life when I feel it is the right time to share my encounters with the Angels and how these meetings have had a profound effect on my life. I now embrace every moment I spend with these very special friends.

Growing up in the era following the Second World War, where everything was cloak and dagger, even among communities and families, I can remember very clearly the day I heard from school friends that the woman, whom I thought was my mother, wasn't my biological parent. I was totally traumatised. This was a woman I loved very dearly and, of course, she loved me and all of our family. Not only did she carry out the motherly duties of caring for us, but she did it with such compassion and love.

I can vividly remember running home as salty tears stung my eyes and streamed down my cheeks. I was so hurt, wondering why anyone would make up such a thing just to cause upset and hurt. I will never forget the look on my mother's face, as I burst through our back door and into the kitchen, to tell my parents what some of the older boys in the village had said. There were three of them, and these boys would later cause me a lot of pain.

My parents were angry and upset and they tried their best to reassure me with comforting words, but as an observant child, I knew it was true. It seemed so very cruel that the woman, whom I loved so dearly, just seemed to be snatched from me. Despite my best efforts, I could not shake off the heaviness in my heart. I was so hurt. I sobbed for days. From that moment on I felt very insecure and anxious. These characteristics overshadowed my true personality, until I reached my early forties.

I was three years old, when my new mother, Christina, and my father came to the orphanage to take me home to join my brothers. Our new mum embraced the job of rearing us. It was at this time I had my first encounter with the Angels. This meeting meant nothing to me at the time; it was only much later in life that the significance of the encounter became crystal clear.

I have vague memories of what conditions in the orphanage were like. Looking back now, I believe the place was shrouded in darkness. It's possible this memory is due to the fact, that during the air raids, no lights were permitted to be on. But, then, I was only a small infant, after all. It was when we were leaving the orphanage that I caught sight of what I now know was, a heavenly being.

On the way up those stone steps from the orphanage, I was in my mother's arms, yet this beautiful, young man seemed to be carrying me. As we reached the top of the steps I remember seeing the black coloured railings. It was the first time I had seen daylight, or a street! There was someone else with us, but I could never put a face to this other person. I know it was a man and I assumed that it was my father. As I got older, and began identifying colours, it struck me how this heavenly being had been surrounded in a bright, white light. He smiled a lot and was very happy. Now, in my autumn years, I am certain that this Angel was Archangel Raphael. That day was also the first time I had met my three brothers and we all settled down to family life. I was very happy. I loved my family.

Another early encounter I can recall vividly was when I was about seven years old. My dad and I were out at the back of the house. Dad was working and I was playing on our swing. My dad had got two pieces of wood and nailed them together and, with a piece of rope, he attached them to two poles. I helped my dad as he hammered in the nails. Ray, my special friend, was beside me. She was as elated as I was! She was clapping and jumping up and down and so was I. I remember being very excited at the prospect of having a swing. When I was a child, toys were very scarce. Ray and I spent many hours on that swing. Very often she would give it a little push to get me started and then sit on my knee. It seemed like we were soaring high into the sky. It was days like that which I treasure the most from my childhood.

It was during one of these carefree days, when Ray, my special friend, and I were on the swing and my dad was busy working in the garden tending to his cherished flowerbeds and vegetables, that Ray said to me: "Come, let's go into the house. Someone wants to see you." I jumped off the swing and, as I followed her into the house, thoughts of who could possibly want to see me, were whizzing through my mind. As I was standing in our kitchen, peering around for this unexpected visitor, I heard a knock on our scullery window. I ran into the scullery and there stood a strange woman. She had a shawl draped around her shoulders, a plain plaid long skirt and long, jet-black hair. I looked at this woman, wondering who she was and where she had come from. Then I spotted Ray standing behind her. As it was unusual for strangers to call at our house, I was a little frightened and unsure at first what to do, but when I saw Ray standing so close to her, my worries melted away. Ray was my best friend and if she felt safe around this strange woman, then I knew there couldn't be any danger.

The woman asked me for a piece of bread. I didn't know what to do. As a child I had always been warned by my parents never to talk to strangers. My head was telling me that I should probably call my father and alert him to this woman's presence, but my heart told me different. There was something about this woman which seemed to draw me to her. I felt sorry for her and I wanted to help in whatever way I could. I decided that I couldn't refuse this woman a piece of bread. I climbed up on the wooden chair which was in our scullery, so I could reach the big, white tin where my mother kept the bread. I took out a piece, buttered it and, because I liked syrup, I put some syrup on it for her too. As I handed it to her, she thanked me, smiled and said: "Your mummy loves you very much."

I was puzzled at this comment because, young as

I was, I knew mammy was in another town working. I also knew that mammy would never say something like that to a stranger. What did she mean? I stood at the window and watched her walk up the path of our house, but not down the lane; she had just disappeared. At that point I began to panic. Where had she gone? I was also afraid that my father would be cross with me for talking to her. I went outside and followed in her footsteps down the path but she was nowhere to be found. I never saw her again.

It would be some years later, when I came across a photograph of my mother, I realised that this lady was indeed, an image of my biological mother. I never spoke of the visit I had from this strange woman. I knew I would get into trouble with my dad if I had mentioned it.

At this stage in my life, the dazzling white light that radiated from this woman meant nothing to me because I had seen it before around others. I took for granted the coloured lights I saw around people's heads. I just assumed that everyone could see them. To me they were part and parcel of life, which indeed they are.

As I grew older, I began to encounter Angels more and more frequently, especially if I happened to waken during the night. My bedroom would be lit up with a big, bright light and always, sitting beside me, would be a heavenly being. They never, ever frightened me; in fact, they always soothed me back to sleep. On these occasions I felt safe and secure.

These occurrences were perfectly normal for me, I

never, ever questioned them. Sometimes I told my mum and dad about them, but they always said the same thing: "It's alright, you've been dreaming." I knew different, however. My eyes were open when I saw them!

4
A RAY OF LIGHT

When I was very young, I didn't quite realise just how extraordinary my special gift was, in fact I didn't realise I even had a gift.

Even though my brothers were much older than me and were not interested in playing with me, as they had their own friends, I was never lost for someone to play with, I always had Ray. Many children have imaginary and make-believe friends but I didn't need to pretend because no matter when I needed companionship my best friend seemed to always appear from nowhere. Her name was Rachel but I called her 'Ray.'

At this point I would like to give you a visual description of my special friend Ray. She was very pretty, with long, black hair which fell into perfect ringlets, like the type of ringlets your mammy, in those days, would have put in your hair overnight with pieces of cloth. She always seemed to be the same height as me. She had slightly paler skin than I had, but it was porcelain-like and her eyes were a dazzling blue, like the colour of the ocean on a clear day and like the ocean, those eyes were always dancing - dancing with joy and, indeed, mischief at times. Ray was so much fun to be with and when she was at my side I always felt more joyful, happy and safe. She was a friend sent from heaven, in other words my Guardian Angel. As a child I was unaware that she was in fact my Guardian Angel. We spent long hours playing together, making mud pies, playing 'wee house' and playing ball against the wall. I shared with her all my childhood secrets. We were forever talking and laughing, just two typical little girls, playing and having fun together.

Some of my fondest memories when growing up are all wrapped up in Ray. When I think back, the thought of Ray still makes me smile. As a little girl, I would often tell my parents of the adventures that Ray and I had, or what we had got up to. It didn't matter if it was fun or mischief, they would always make the same remark about how vivid my imagination was. I suppose I never really understood what they meant and I could never understand why they never paid any attention to Ray.

One incident which stands out very clearly from my play years with Ray, occurred just a few days before Christmas. Every year, my brothers and I hung one of my dad's thick, woolly socks on the fireplace for when Santa would visit. This particular year, I decided that I would hang up two socks - one for me and one for Ray. I remember my mammy warning me: "Now, don't be greedy or Santa won't leave you anything!" I protested and told her that I wasn't being greedy. I explained that the extra stocking was for Ray. At that, my mum got quite upset and said: "There you go again, pretending there is someone else around." Despite my mother's warning, I hung up a stocking for Ray. On Christmas morning I couldn't understand why Santa hadn't left her anything. That made me sad. However, Santa had left me a packet of balloons, along with an apple, an orange and a box of bubbles, so I shared my goodies with Ray.

Ray and I spent many, long, happy days together. She was my constant companion, along with Pat, my dog and Fluff, my cat. When I went to school, Ray never came but everyday, when I got out of school and walked up the street, there at the top of the hill, were Ray and Pat, patiently waiting for me. I was always so pleased to see them and we would all run home together.

One day my mother sent me to town for a message. As a little treat she said that I could buy something for myself. I ran as fast as my little legs could carry me in to town. After delivering my mother's message, I called into the local newsagents. This was a rare opportunity as I didn't often get special treats like this, so I took my time in deciding what exactly I was going to spend my money on. My mouth watered as my eyes feasted upon the different varieties of sweets laid out before me but, as it was such a beautiful, sunny day, I decided on an ice-cream, topped with strawberry sauce.

I was very content as I walked home licking my ice-cream. I wasn't too far from home when a black, shiny motorcar came driving down the road. Now, in those days motor cars, especially expensive ones like this one, were very rare. The car slowed down as it approached me and then came to a stop. There was a man and a woman in the car and they called me over. As I was talking to them I noticed the car's stylish, red interior. Red was my favourite colour. I didn't recognise the man or the woman, but they appeared to be very friendly. They offered me a ride home. My house wasn't very far away, but the thought of having a spin in such a fancy motorcar excited me. I was just about to climb into the car when Ray suddenly appeared at my side. She nudged me on the back and told me to come with her. When the lady saw me hesitate she held out a three-pence piece and sweets, which were very tempting. Again, Ray nudged me, but harder this time, and without questioning it, I somehow knew to turn and run with Ray. I never saw the car, or the people who were in it, again.

In those days, I didn't believe that there was much danger for children, but perhaps there was and we just never heard about it. To this day, I don't know if there was anything sinister about the couple in the motorcar. I'm just glad that Ray happened to turn up when she did. Obviously, Ray was more aware than I was, of the danger that may have been lurking beneath the surface of these two people's invitation to come with them.

*

School for me was fine for the first two or three years. It was a beautiful, old, red-brick building which had quite a lot of character. I loved learning, but I just never felt that I fitted in with my classmates. Somehow, I knew I was different. I often wished that I could just be like everyone else.

My first two years passed off peacefully, but it was when I was halfway through my third year that the trouble started. As some of the children got older and realised that there was something different about me, the bullying started - not from my classmates, but three older boys in the school.

I felt safe while in the classroom, because I was aware that the headmaster in the school appeared to be keeping an eye on everyone and I did have some good friends in my class. It was during the breaks and lunchtimes that the bullies were at their worst. I was terrified of them, probably because they were much older than me. So, I usually tried to hide out in the girls' toilets, not the most hygienic of hiding places, but it was the only place I felt safe.

In the beginning, some of the girls in my class felt sorry for me, so they joined me in the toilets and we chatted and played quite happily. We drew out hopscotch on the floor and remained there until the master rang the big, hand bell. When it sounded, we knew it was time to return to class. However, it wasn't long before the teachers discovered our hiding place. When this happened, my two playmates and I were ordered out of the toilets by our teacher and into the classroom, where she questioned us about our meetings in the toilets. As she towered above us, I felt as if I had done something wrong, when really all I was doing was protecting myself.

Each one of us told the truth about the hair pulling, the hitting and the tripping of me by the boys, but instead of punishing the culprits, the teacher sent the other two children away and chastised me. She pulled out her cane and, as she counted out each one of her five slaps, it took all my strength not to run home and never come back. I had never been slapped at school before, by any of the teachers, and I was very upset. After all, I had done nothing wrong. I remember wondering why my teacher couldn't see that I was the innocent victim, but no matter how much I pleaded with her, she wouldn't believe me. As far as she was concerned, I was the troublemaker. My hands stung bitterly for hours. but I wouldn't let her see me cry. I never complained about the bullying again.

As I was forbidden from hiding in the toilets, I had no choice but to play in the playground with the rest of the children. I tried my best to rise above it. I used to try and shut out their hurtful words and ignore their comments, but it didn't always work. It still hurt but I was more afraid of the physical abuse. I hoped that if I didn't answer back they would get bored with me and move on. But, as the weeks and months rolled by, the bullying continued. Some of the injuries I sustained during this time included a broken tooth, black eyes and many cuts and bruises. I tried to hide the bullies' marks from my parents as best I could but sometimes it was just too difficult.

Saturday night was bath night in our house and mammy used to fill our big, tin bath with water and she bathed me in front of our Stanley range. On a few occasions at bath time, she saw the marks and she asked me how I had sustained these particular injuries, but I always had an answer. I would say that I had fallen off my swing or that I had tripped over while I was running in the playground. I felt guilty lying to my mum, but I was so desperately afraid that, if I told her the truth, it would only make things worse. I knew that if my dad found out, he would go straight down to the school to confront our teacher and then I would end up getting another whipping. I was also afraid of what the bullies would do to me if I told on them, so I said nothing and continued on as best I could.

Because I was considered to be different, I had only a few friends at school, and as the bullying continued, I had even fewer friends. Naturally, any of the girls who had befriended me, began to distance themselves from me when the bullies were around. They, too, were afraid of being targeted by this bullying gang. Most of my school days were spent alone, always looking over my shoulder. As I grew older, I realised that the correct procedure would have been, not only to tell someone, but to tell everyone!

It wasn't long before the bullying escalated. I didn't understand some of the names the boys were beginning to call me. All I knew was that I must be to blame in some way, for who I was. I felt very sad, but as always, my friend, Ray, was there to cheer me up.

*

One summer's evening, while in the park with my two school friends, a gang of bigger boys came along. Immediately, they started calling me names. Before I knew it, they had grabbed me. I tried to fight back as best I could. I kicked out and tried to struggle free, but they had such a tight grip of me, there was absolutely nothing I could do. They dragged me further and further into the nearby woods. At this point, I scanned the woods for Ray, but she wasn't around. The boys had some sort of twine with them, and with this, they began to tie me to a tree. They also tied my feet together and my hands behind my back. By this stage, my school friends were long gone. The boys gathered sticks and leaves and put them around me. One of the boys had matches, and they managed to get a fire started and the flames began to flicker around my feet. I shouted for help, but there was no one around. The bullies were chanting obscene slogans. It was the first time I had heard the "F" word. As the small pile of leaves and twigs began to smoke and burn, my sandals and socks started to turn black. Then, in the midst of the smoke, a clearing came, and what I can only describe as the most beautiful young woman, appeared before my eyes. She said: "Don't cry little one, help is on the way."

I couldn't take my eyes off this woman. The dress that she wore was pure white and she was practically glowing. She also seemed to be standing above the ground. I think this was the first time I realised, that no one else was seeing, what I was in the habit of seeing. One could say this was a new dawn for many more phenomena which I was to encounter in my lifetime. That was the day I knew, for sure, I was different, and in a way it saddened me.

This heavenly being stayed with me until a neighbouring woman came into the woods calling for her son who, I might add, was not part of the bullying gang. As soon as she appeared, all the boys ran away. She managed to catch one of them and she smacked him. She put the fire out and untied me and told me not to tell my dad. I ran home, intending to tell my mum about what had happened, but when I arrived home, she scolded me for getting my socks and sandals dirty. Somehow, I wasn't able to tell her because she was shouting so much, so I said nothing. I have often wondered why Ray didn't come to the rescue, but perhaps, it was her, as

Angels can appear in different guises.

Understandably, at this young age in my life, my confidence was at an all time low. The other children, with the exception of two or three, didn't seem to be able to accept me because of who I was. Perhaps, they too, were afraid of the bullies. Later, when my dad came in from work, my mum told him how I had been in the muck and he also scolded me. I answered him back by saying: "The lady knows I wasn't in the muck." That evening my dad took me aside and told me not to make up any more of these stories. He said: "People will say that there is something odd about you."

In his own way, I know that my dad was trying to protect me. From that day on, I kept all my little secrets to myself - like seeing the lovely coloured lights over people's heads and all the times I talked to, what I know now, are Angels.

An artist's impression of the Angel who appeared to Gwen when bullies tied her up and attempted to set her on fire.

*

The next big event I recall, was when I was about seven years old. It was coming up to Halloween, and some of my school friends and I were in the park playing. At this point, I was beginning to see less and less of Ray. I remember it was such a bright, clear, cold day. The sun was shining, illuminating the colourful display of orange, red and gold autumn leaves on the trees. My friends and I were having a lovely time. We were off school for mid-term break and I didn't have to worry about the bullies, or so I thought. Next thing, we heard the squeal and the bang of squibs (fireworks). The bigger boys in our school, the ones who we had hoped to avoid, were there and they were setting off squibs. We played on, but it wasn't long before they spied me. They came closer to our group and started calling me names. Some of my school friends shouted at them to leave me alone, but one of the boys grabbed me and held me down until another set a squib on top of my head. He had just lit it when, out of nowhere, appeared Ray. She seemed to blow on the squib and it fizzled out and then she was gone and so was everyone else!

*

Bullying occurs in all walks of life and can touch everyone no matter where they are. It appears it has now reached epidemic proportions. This is in no small way a result of technological advances, cyber bullying being an example. It occurs in some of our schools, the work place and also in our communities, as well as happening in some people's homes.

It is well-known that bullies are cowards who feel inadequate within themselves. These cowardly people, who seek worldly power, attack those who they believe are the weaker people in society. The results of this can have a very devastating effect on people and, at times, have a sad ending for the victim. Most people, at some point in their lives, will suffer at the hands of bullies and will be left feeling isolated and hurt, which can lead on to serious consequences.

If you have been bullied, please speak with someone you trust, a family member or a friend. Do not keep it a secret; tell everyone if you have to, until someone listens to you. Often exposure of the bullying can alleviate the situation.

Do not suffer in silence.

If someone confides in you that they are being bullied, listen seriously to what they are saying, as it takes a lot of courage to come forward and admit to being bullied. Offer support and try to work together to find a solution.

Always remember you are special, unique and a strong person and you don't deserve to be bullied. No one has the right to tell you otherwise.

When I was around seven years old, I fell violently ill and had to be taken in an ambulance to the local hospital to have my appendix removed. Back then, a surgical procedure, such as this, meant a long stay in hospital. I don't think I will ever forget the trauma of that experience and the distress of being separated from my family. It terrified me! I thought I would never see my family again. Every time the nurses wheeled in their trolley, I screamed and screamed. All those needles and things frightened me. I was so sad and lonely and I cried constantly, especially at night. All I wanted was to be back home with my family.

One evening, I was so distressed that one of the nurses actually slapped me, which, of course only made things worse. As I lay in bed, sobbing into my pillow, an amazing, heavenly being appeared at my side. He called me by my name and his soothing voice immediately calmed me and my tears stopped. I had never seen anyone like him before. He had such a kind-looking face and was dressed in a long, flowing, white robe. He appeared to be much taller than my daddy. He didn't tell me his name and I never asked him. I just called him 'Mister.' He came back every night and held my hand as I fell asleep. When I awoke in the morning, he was gone.

Somehow, the rest of my stay in hospital wasn't quite so bad. It was only when I was much older, that I realised that this man was an Angel, who had come to my aid, to comfort me. When this struck me, I didn't know what to think!

One afternoon, my mum and dad came to see me in hospital and it wasn't long before they got talking to the lovely lady who was beside me in the ward. She told them that I was a 'great little girl, full of imagination,' and that I was 'forever talking to myself, especially at night.' The second time that my mum and dad came, my older brother Denis came to visit me too and, at last, my friend Ray came with them. I was delighted to see her. I missed her so much. I told her about the nice gentleman who came every night and sat with me until I fell asleep. Ray asked me his name. I told her I had asked and he had just smiled, so I called him 'Mister.' Ray seemed to understand. During this conversation with Ray, I heard my dad say to the lady beside me: "Yes, I see what you mean when you say she talks to herself. She does it all the time." At least *I* knew I wasn't talking to myself; I was talking to Ray.

When I came home from the hospital, Ray was waiting for me, but I wasn't allowed outside. She only played with me inside our house, when everyone else was busy. One day, I asked my mammy to give Ray some dinner too. I got scolded and I knew never to mention Ray again. I was scared that my parents would send her away. I shared my worries with Ray, but she said that she would never leave me. However, that was the last time that she came in to our house. Soon, I was better and was able to join Ray outside, and we spent many more happy days playing together.

*

A few months after my operation, our parish priest arrived at our house and announced that it was time that I made my First Holy Communion. Because I went to a school that was of a different persuasion, I was unable to make my Holy Communion with the rest of the children from our parish. This lovely priest explained to me that I was very special and that I would make my First Confession and First Holy Communion on the first Sunday of the month, rather than on the second Sunday, which was known as "Children's Sunday." I hadn't a clue what he was talking about, but I was looking forward to seeing what all the fuss was about. I was given new prayers to learn, which my mum and my brother Denis taught me. I practised them every night. It wasn't long before the very special day arrived. I had been given a smart new coat which had been made from my mum's old coat. I got a pair of new sandals and a new bonnet.

As we walked to Mass that Sunday morning, I felt proud of my new clothes and I remember wishing that Ray would come to see my new outfit. On our way to the chapel, my mum and dad went to great lengths to explain to me that no other children would be making their Holy Communion except for me. Again, this made me feel very special.

When we arrived at the Church, the priest was outside waiting for us. He took me into this strange box and I knelt down and told him my sins, which my mum and brother had told me to say. At that time, Mass was said in Latin and was very long. As a child, I had no idea what it was all about. At some point during the Mass, my mum whispered to me that it was time for me to go up and kneel on the altar, to receive the Body of Christ. I went along with her and did what she did. I put my hands under the white cloth and, whilst waiting for the priest to come to me, I looked up onto the altar. It was then I saw them - rows and rows of children, all dressed in the same attire as myself! They were smiling down at me and, in the middle of them all, was Ray!

When we came down to our seat, I was so excited. I kept saying to my mum: "But the children are all here, even Ray!" My mum kept telling me to keep quiet, so I turned to my dad and told him. He smiled and said: "I thought this had all stopped!" I was bewildered and I couldn't understand why they couldn't see the children.

After Mass, the priest took us home in his car and I told him about all the children on the altar. He didn't seem to hear me. Again, my mum told me to keep quiet. When we got back to our house and we were having tea, the priest gave me half a crown. My dad exchanged it for a three-pence-piece and I was allowed to go to the shop for ice-cream. I felt very special that day. Not only was I allowed ice-cream, but so many children had come, with Ray, to join me on the day of my First Holy Communion!

Gwen is pictured here on her First Holy Communion Day in 1949.

5
HOME AT LAST

On the 11th June 1954, we moved from Hillsborough to the country. I was only twelve years old and I took to my new home in Draperstown, like a duck to water.

I remember that day so vividly, as we drove into Draperstown from Magherafelt. I immediately noticed that the beautiful Sperrin Mountains seemed to have a different and glorious hue of colour. The mountain gorse was in full bloom, displaying a strong, yellow colour, glistening in the sun. As we neared the mountains, there was a sprinkling of dwellings where some of the locals lived. The closer we came to the mountains, the more I could see the animals that dwelt there as well - sheep and lambs seemed to be everywhere!

I suppose, from a spiritual perspective, life was uneventful, but in a physical sense, my life really began in Draperstown. When we first drove into that small, market town in the foothills of the mountains, my thought was: "I am home!" A feeling of contentment and ease washed over me. I may have only been a young girl, but something told me that this would be the place where I would remain for the rest of my life.

People were friendly in our new hometown and the bullying was finally over. As a family, we settled into our new home very quickly. Ray came with us and, of course, Fluff, my cat, came too! For the best part of five years, life was good. For the first time in my life, I looked forward to going to school. There was a great sense of freedom from the torment that the bullies had inflicted upon me for so long. I began to feel more confident. Yes, life had definitely changed for the better!

In those days, the town school was located at St. Patrick's Street, in the building which is now one of the local supermarkets. Back then, it had white-washed walls and a slate roof. I loved going out to school in the mornings. I loved learning and playing with my new friends. School life, back then, was very different. Whilst we used pencils to complete most of our schoolwork, we used steel-nibbed pens, dipped in ink, for essays or compositions, as they were called back then. We had to take extra care not to blot our work or else we would receive a scolding, from the master or mistress, for sloppiness. The girls and boys were separated at break times, so there were two playgrounds, one for the boys and one for the girls. As I got used to my new school, I felt, at last, that I belonged. I made many good friends, friends who are still an important part of my life today. Eventually, Ray disappeared, but by this stage, I had figured out that she was not of this world. Little did I know, though, that many years later, we would meet again.

*

As I reached my teenage years, I left behind my childish ways and it wasn't long before I wanted my own independence and freedom. It was fortunate that my parents seemed to understand this and I was given little liberties every now and then. During these years, my friends and I would have often spent many long and blissful evenings on the banks of the majestic Moyola River. That was our secret hide-away. For my fourteenth birthday, my parents bought me a blue bike. I couldn't believe my luck!

My friends and I spent many happy hours cycling around the mountain trails. Most of the time we had to take turns as there were only a few bikes between us all, but sure that was all part of the fun. We called with ,many local people who sometimes treated us to soda bread, hot off the griddle, or ice-cold lemonade, or buttermilk. Another favourite pastime of ours, was getting up early in the mornings and sitting on the rooftops watching the sun rising. Reflecting back on those days, and, the special memories we made together, make me very happy.
The years soon marched on, and it wasn't long before the time came for me, to either leave school and take up employment, or to continue my studies at a secondary school.

I desperately wanted to stay on at school and continue with my education but, in those days, decisions were made for us. The nearest secondary school was St. Mary's Convent in Magherafelt, which would have meant a bus journey for me. Being the youngest in the family, and the only girl, my father was always very protective of me. I suppose it was only natural, given the fact that he had been separated from me for over three years while fighting in the war. He had also lost two children and a young wife, so the idea of me travelling, on a bus every day, didn't sit very well with him. So, when I turned fifteen, I had to leave school. I went straight into one of the local clothing factories. My job was sewing cuffs on to the sleeves of shirts. I didn't particularly enjoy my work, but it was a job, and I was earning a wage, which meant I could occasionally treat myself to the latest fashion and music. I have absolutely no regrets, nor do I hold any ill feeling towards my father's decision about my education. He thought it was the right decision at the time and I respect that.

During my adolescent years, I was a typical teenager. I was interested in the latest rock and roll music, makeup, fashions and, of course, boys! I had taken a fancy to one of the local lads, and it wasn't long before I had fallen head-over-heels in love with him. This was the boy I was later to marry.

At this point in my life, the only psychic experiences I was having, were nightmarish dreams and flashes. Some of the visions I had were terrifying but I didn't dwell on them too much. I put them to the back of my mind.

For the first time, I seemed to fit in with my peers and I wasn't going to let anything jeporadise my friendships. Besides, I had much better things to be doing.

*

As a family, we had all adjusted quite easily to our new life and the years seemed to just slip by. We had been living in Draperstown, for just over five years, when my mum was sent into hospital for a routine operation. It was during her stay in hospital, that I had a terrible dream. It's a dream that still haunts me to this day. I dreamt that it was my wedding day, but when I entered the church I could see myself walking up the aisle in a black, lace dress. All the guests were my own family and they, too, were dressed in black, right down to the black carnation flowers as button holes. As I walked up the aisle, I noticed a coffin beside the altar. In my dream, I thought: "Why is there a funeral in the church on my wedding day?" As I reached the altar, the groom turned to face me, but it was not my boyfriend, it was my brother, Desmond. In the dream, I panicked and said to him: "I can't marry you, you are my brother!" I then woke up in a cold sweat, with my heart racing. I had experienced many strange dreams over the years, but this particular dream really upset me. There was something sinister about this one, so I mentioned it to my dad the following morning. As usual, he tried to reassure me that it was only a dream. On his advice, I tried to forget about it but, no matter what I did, the dream seemed to be at the back of my mind, niggling me.

A few days later, my fears were realised. My dad was at the hospital visiting my mum, while I was at home, with my, then, boyfriend, when a knock came to our door. I went to the door and opened it, to find a policeman standing on the doorstep. He asked for my dad and I told him that he was at the hospital. I sensed that something dreadful had happened and I asked him if everything was ok. The policeman told me that my brother, Desmond, had been involved in an accident, but he assured me he was alright. I was so relieved. It was some time before my dad returned home and I wasted no time in rushing out to tell him what had happened. As I set eyes on my father's ashen face, I knew, before he even spoke, that everything was not ok. Something dreadful had happened. My gut feeling was right. My twenty-one year old bother, Desmond had been killed in a tragic road accident.

Things were never the same in our home again. My brother's death was the first time that I had to deal with losing someone close to me. A few days after the funeral, my dad asked me about the dream that I had. When I told him that the brother I dreamt I was marrying was now dead, it shocked him certainly, but it also seemed, for the first time that he was taking me seriously. After this, my father no longer treated me like a child, but as the adult that I was.

Before my mum was discharged from hospital, my father sat me down at our kitchen table and told me that there were things he needed to tell me. He began by reminding me of the children at school, who had told me that my biological mother was dead. It was then that he told me that this was in fact true. He told me that my mum had died when I was just six-months old, and she was just thirty-six. He then went on to tell me that I had a sister who had died when she was just three years old. This had happened before I was born. Next, he told me that I had another, older, brother called George, who had been killed in the Second World War, when he was eighteen years old. I can still remember my father lying across the table, with his head in his hands, sobbing uncontrollably. He told me that he was tired of life. He had lost a brother of just eighteen in the First World War, his parents, two sons, a daughter, and his beloved, young wife. He was so sad, but I was too young and inexperienced to comprehend the deep grief my father was experiencing, and I knew no way of consoling him.

I went to bed that night, a very sombre, young girl but, somehow, I came to realise that this was a wake-up call as to what life is really about on Earth. I knelt at my bedside and prayed to God to give me enlightenment, as to how to comfort my father in his deep grief. Warm tears flowed down my cheeks. I was sad for the loss of a brother, but sadder, for my father, who seemed to have given up all hope. It was then that my attention was drawn to a strange aroma which seemed to be everywhere in the room. I lifted my head up and, upon my bed, I saw the most amazing sight! Before me was a vision of three heavenly beings! They were surrounded by roses of every colour. I, somehow, knew these heavenly beings had come to give me guidance. The smallest of the three, then spoke to me. She said: "Gwendoline, do not be afraid. We are here to help you fulfill your task on Earth, which God has set out for you."

Somehow, from that moment on, I was able to find the words to console my father and we comforted each other. I felt that this helped to forge an even greater bond between us.

*

Nine months later, my beloved dad started to lose weight and was making a lot of trips to the doctors' surgery. I wasn't told he was ill and I didn't ask. I suppose, a part of me was afraid of what I would hear. It was around this time, that one night, I was walking down our hall. My parents had already gone to bed, so I was startled when I heard a very loud crash. I searched around the kitchen, and other rooms, but nothing seemed to be out of place. I went on to bed and I was just getting ready to go to sleep when, all of a sudden, my bedroom lit up with a massive, white light. In the centre of this light was

a heavenly being. The man spoke to me and said: "You are going to lose someone very close to you. God is taking this person, whom you love, home."
Within a few moments the light and the being were gone. In the morning I omitted to mention the Angel's visit to my parents. I thought it best not to worry them, but I certainly was very worried and upset, but I kept it hidden.

*

As time went on, the trips to the Doctors' surgery became more frequent for my beloved father, and he had to make quite a few visits to the local hospital. At no time did mum or dad mention to me why daddy was making all these visits to the surgery, and I didn't ask, possibly because, deep down, I knew. Frequently, I thought about the message I had received from the Angel. The illness had begun in June 1960 , and in February of 1961, dad peacefully passed away. It turned out that he was very ill and doctors could offer him no form of treatment.

Following my brother's death, my dad and I had become even closer, so I struggled to cope with his passing. Now, I was dealing with the loss of my dad, and trying to be there for my mum, who was not coping very well. For my Mum and me, life seemed to have lost all its sweetness. Dad was the main provider for our family. When he died, we were forced to leave the house we lived in, the quaint little cottage that had once been such a happy home. My mum tried her best to keep positive, but she was very lonely, and for me, I just missed my dad. I cried myself to sleep most nights. It seemed that, within a few short weeks, our world had crashed in around us. We tried to find a new home in Draperstown but, in those days, accommodation was scarce. Sadly, we had no other choice but to return to our former village, where we lived with my brother, Graham, for a few months. Mum found it hard to accept life as it was, but, eventually, she got a house of her own, and then, six months later, I was married and I returned to Draperstown. I was very happy, as I was able to visit my dad's grave every day and mum spent a lot of time visiting us, mostly at weekends.

6
LIFE'S GREATEST BLESSINGS

Francis took my hand in marriage on the 8th January 1963. This was one of the happiest days of my life. I was marrying the love of my life.

On the morning of my wedding, the snow was falling heavily and the ground was a blanket of white. I was desperately sad that my father wasn't there to share my special day. I still missed him so much, but one blessing I can thank my father for, was taking me to Draperstown, which enabled me to follow my life path on Earth, and meet Francis. My brother, Graham, gave me away, and my loving mother and all my family, along with my new husband's family gathered around. I will forever cherish the happy memories of that day.

Gwen and Francis are pictured on their Wedding Day, 8th January, 1963.

Married life began for my husband and me, as it does for any other young couple. It took us a few years to find our feet and adjust to one another, but we were very much in love and we were both very happy. I felt secure at last.

We built our family home, which is the very same house I live in today. My relationship with my husband's mother was brilliant; she seemed to understand me. She was such a laid-back, generous and pleasant woman to know. People would often say she was a saint and, indeed, I would agree entirely. She was like a second mother to me. On one occasion, she told me I was 'like a breath of fresh air.' I took it as a compliment, even though I had no idea what she was talking about.

In the early years of our marriage, I once again began to experience flashes and visions. At times, these flashes were quite disturbing. I often had visions of horrific road accidents and train crashes. I also saw apparitions of people dying in other countries, not only from starvation, but as a result of ongoing conflicts and war situations. I also had many nightmares relating to natural disasters. My husband told me that, on many occasions, I would wake up in the night, speaking in a foreign language. I always wondered, afterwards, if this was because of the amount of travelling I did during my dreams. We all travel in our dreams every night, but some of us don't remember anything about it.

*

After twelve months of blissful married life, we were blessed with a baby boy. The day that our first son, Peter, was born was one of the happiest days of my life. I will never forget the moment that I first set eyes on him. I was filled with a deep love. It is a love that I share for all my sons and it is just like God's love for us – endless!

Like all new parents, it took some time getting used to being completely responsible for a tiny little baby, but Francis and I soon got used to it. A year and a half later, in 1965, another beautiful son was born. We called him Kevin. We felt very blessed. Life was busy, but it was set to get even busier. In 1967 we were blessed with our third beautiful son, we called him Stephen. Another of God's blessings came along in 1971; our fourth beautiful son, Conrad, was born. Our fifth beautiful son, Philip, was born in 1980. Life was busy, but we were immensely happy as a family.

We have so many happy memories, as does most families, of when our children were growing up. We have precious memories of the different stages of their childhood: the first tooth, the first step, the first day at school, the long, winter nights cuddled up at the blazing fire, telling little jokes, watching the children's programmes and playing board games. Ludo was a popular game in our home, and the one we had the most arguments about, but that's what made it all the more fun. In the summer, we spent a lot of time outdoors. Davagh Forest was a regular venue for us. The boys loved it! We all played many, different games and paddled in the small river. Later, when they got older, football was introduced to the fun and games. I sat there and watched their daddy play with them, and I thanked God for our family, and how happy we all were. Many trips were made to Portstewart Beach, and we always came home with a car full of sand, and very tired boys. Later, we holidayed in Donegal and, again, much fun and enjoyment was had by all. Of all the good memories I have, these are the most precious.

Gwen and Francis are pictured with their five sons: Kevin, Stephen, Conrad, Peter and Philip.

Shortly after the birth of our son, Conrad, my husband, decided to start his own business, a home bakery. I always admired Francis' courage. Launching your own business, at anytime, is a big step, but when you had four young mouths to feed, it was an even bigger risk. However, Francis was confident and sure that it would work, and I had no reason to doubt him. I supported him one hundred per cent. Francis put in a lot of hard work and made many sacrifices to get the business up and running. Thankfully, it all paid off and he made a great success of it.

*

Whenever there was an opportunity, my husband and I loved to go fishing together. We always found it incredibly peaceful and serene, sitting by the side of the river, listening to the gentle flow of the current, whilst waiting for a catch.

As a child, I went on many fishing expeditions with my dad and brothers, and on a Sunday, mum joined us too. My dad had a big, black, tar boat with two oars. During the holidays, weather permitting, we would set off with all our fishing gear. Mum always prepared a picnic for us which she packed into her big, wicker basket, which she hooked under her arm, and we'd set off to the lake. Our picnics usually consisted of some bread and jam, or cheese, or whatever food my mum had in the house. In those days, 'niceties' were in short supply. We would pile into my dad's boat and row out to the middle of the lake, where my dad and my older brother would throw out their lines in the hope that we would catch something for our evening tea. I, on the other hand, had my very own fishing rod - a lump of wood with a piece of string and hook attached! I felt very important, having my own specially-made fishing rod. Basically, my dad had made the rod to try and keep me occupied during our fishing expeditions. This is one of my happiest memories, when living in Hillsborough.

I must have been five years old when my dad first taught me how to fish. For a period, in my late teens, I gave it up, but in later years, when I reached my late thirties, I got the bug for fishing again.

In the early years of our marriage, when I decided to go fishing, my husband was dubious about letting me go on my own and he was right. Being close to the water has its own dangers. So, to keep his mind at ease, he would come along with me. He often would have taken a book or the newspaper with him, something to keep him occupied. However, that all changed one Sunday afternoon. I was sitting by the river hoping for a catch, when I had to make a trip back to the car. I asked Francis if he would hold my fishing-rod until I returned. When I came back, a few minutes later, I was surprised to see that he had managed to catch a brown trout! I will never forget the look on his face. He was beaming with pleasure. It seemed that, during that fishing trip, Francis had got the bug for fishing too. The following day, he went out and bought himself a fishing-rod and fishing soon became something we enjoyed doing together. It allowed us a break away from our busy home and working life, and gave us the opportunity to reflect on whatever was going on, at that point, in our lives.

Over the years, we travelled the length and breadth of Ireland, fishing on many rivers. We had an amazing time, and I have some wonderful memories from our trips, that I treasure to this day. It is amazing to think that it all began on a black, tar boat on Hillsborough Lake!

7
SIGNS FROM THE ANGELS

Once our home bakery business was up and running, Francis and I decided to launch ourselves into the local music scene. My husband was a fantastic musician. He could play many different instruments but he was exceptionally talented on the trumpet. He was a member of the Granada Show Band and the Northern Swing Band. They travelled all around Ireland. On one occasion they even travelled to Cork to appear on the Hughie Green television show.

This is the first show band that Francis performed with, known as the Granada Show Band.

Francis was also a member of the Northern Swing Band. Here they are performing on the Hughie Green television show.

I, on the other hand, was a country and western singer, so we decided to combine our talents. We figured that, if we played a few gigs at the weekend, it would help towards paying off the debt we had incurred on the outlay of equipment for the business. With our four sons, the family business and our music, life was hectic. We could never have managed any of it without the support of my family, especially my mother. She was a tower of strength. Reflecting back on those times, we were doing all this travelling around the different venues at a very dangerous time in Northern Ireland. The troubles were rife. We put in long hours between our two jobs, but, surprisingly, even though I had experienced many flashes of the bombings and killings in the mid-seventies, it didn't deter me from going on the road. I knew my husband needed my support and that was enough for me.

Most of our gigs were held locally but, in those days, nowhere was safe. Many times, when we were travelling late at night, we would be stopped and interrogated by members of the Royal Ulster Constabulary (RUC). It was on occasions like this, that the danger we faced was really brought home. Of course, I was frightened, but I prayed to God and the Angels for their protection. Indeed, we had a few lucky, or Angelic, escapes during our time on the road.

One night, in particular, I had a horrifying dream. I had a vision that I was standing on a staircase which appeared to be made from glass bottles. I didn't recognise the building that I was standing in, but, as I looked at my feet, I noticed a small parcel. I bent down to pick it up, but, as I lifted the package, smoke started to pour from it. I dropped the parcel and I knew that I had to escape. As I turned to run back down the steps, the air around me was thick with smoke. I could no longer see the steps under my feet. I stumbled and grabbed the banister. I screamed for my husband but he didn't come. I don't know if the package exploded in the dream or not, but I was jolted awake in a cold sweat. My heart was pounding and my body was trembling all over. I tried telling myself that it was only a dream, but there was something very sinister and real about this one.

In the past, Angels had communicated with me through my dreams. So, my initial feeling was that something awful was going to happen. I shared my worries with my very practical and logical husband. He tried to reassuring me that it was only a dream and I tried to take comfort from his words. But in the back of mind, I knew the Angels were warning me of something.

Two weeks later, we were playing a gig in a neighbouring town. The pub we were performing in, was one of the few, which I remember, that had stairs. We were all set up and ready-to-roll, when I remembered I had a message to do in the downstairs bar. As I walked down, I noticed a bag sitting on the stairs. I stepped over it, and went into the lower bar.

I thought someone must have dropped the bag, perhaps they were looking for it, so I mentioned it to the owner. His reaction was totally unexpected. He flew into a blind panic and immediately ran to call the police. It was at that moment that I remembered my dream. Within a few minutes, the bar owner got me out by the back door and down to the basement, where his brother lived. Luckily enough, there was a trapdoor from the upper bar down to the basement. Very quickly, my husband dropped our music equipment down into the basement, along with himself and a few other patrons. We were able to access the street through a side door. We jumped into our car and sped off. About half an hour later the package, which was a viable bomb, exploded, totally destroying the premises. Fortunately, that night, everyone managed to escape unharmed.

Later, as I lay in bed, I thought about the near escape we all had. Just at that moment, an emerald green light lit up our bedroom. At first, I didn't understand it. Then it seemed as though I heard a soft voice in my heart say: "I am watching over you both my child; there is much work for you to do." The green light remained in the room. At times, I was able to make out an Angelic face in the light, but at some point, I fell asleep, and when I awoke in the morning, the light was gone. I felt peaceful and protected.

*

Some months later, we had a similar close encounter. We had been booked to play in a bar in a town, about thirty miles from our home village. We had never played a gig there before, so we wanted to get there early. We were quite near our destination when, all of a sudden, the inside of our car was lit up by a bright, white light. I was startled, because I knew my husband was oblivious to it. He just kept on driving. I didn't understand the meaning of the light so I didn't know what to do. I tried to figure out what the Angels were trying to tell me. I was in two minds about telling my husband when a stern voice interrupted my thoughts, and said: "Turn around and go home!" My blood ran cold. This was another divine intervention. I cried out to my husband to stop the car and turn back home. He was very confused at my sudden change of mind. He kept asking me why, but I wasn't entirely sure what to tell him. He then became very angry and protested that we couldn't let these people down by not turning up. I knew that to cancel at the last minute was bad for business and it would certainly do us harm, but I was adamant that I was not going.

By this time, my husband had stopped the car and had got out to stand at the roadside. Francis was determined to try and persuade me to change my mind. I knew that he wouldn't give up unless I told him what I had seen and heard. As soon as I repeated the words I had heard, I didn't have to say anything else. He immediately turned the car and headed back home.

A few minutes later, we travelled through a small village and my husband stopped the car close to a telephone box, where he made a call to the gentleman who had booked us. My husband made some excuse, but the man was not pleased. He told us that we would never get another booking from him. Unfortunately, for him, he was right. Just hours later, the bar was targeted in a paramilitary attack, leaving several injured.

News of this terrible incident, once again, brought home to me the danger that people faced daily, during the troubled times in Northern Ireland. My emotions were in turmoil. I felt very sad and frightened, but also relieved and thankful that one of my heavenly beings had come to save us. Deep down, I knew it was God's plan, but it still haunted me for a long time afterwards.

During this period in my life, I experienced many dreams and flashes relating to the bombings and killings in Northern Ireland. Sadly, most of these resulted in many fatalities and serious injuries. I was too frightened to go to the police with the information I had from these premonitions. At that time, I thought they might suspect that I had some 'inside information,' which, of course, I hadn't.

*

Another very vivid dream that I had, around that time, still haunts me to this very day. It was about a little child being abducted.

It was a Friday night; we had been out late performing at a gig. I had been only sleeping for a few hours when I woke up in a state of sheer panic. In my vision I saw a child being snatched and taken away in a large vehicle. I can even remember seeing the perpetrator's face. The child, in the dream, was close to the age of our son, Conrad. I was terrified that the dream was a warning to me that something terrible was going to happen to him. For the whole of the next day, I wouldn't let any of the boys out of my sight. They sensed that something was annoying me so they did as they were told, much to my relief. The following morning, which was a Sunday, Francis and I sat down together to read the Sunday papers. As I glanced at the front page story, I almost collapsed with shock! There, on the front page, was the beautiful, smiling face of the little child in my dream, who had been abducted the previous day.

I read the story, and as the words sank in, I felt sick. Everything in my nightmare had come true. I knew this little, innocent child was in grave danger. I was so upset and distressed that I felt my only choice was to contact a priest, who was a family friend, but it took a lot of courage to do so. I told him about my dream but I'm not sure he believed me. He promised to pass the information on to the police but I never heard another word about it.

Still, to this day, I feel I should have tried harder to do something more to rescue the young child, yet I had no idea how to go about it at that time.

*

In 1978, I fell seriously ill and was rushed into hospital, where I spent three weeks. My doctors were puzzled as to what this mysterious illness was and, because they couldn't identify it, they didn't know how to treat it. Therefore I received no treatment. During my time in hospital, I was isolated into a small, side ward on my own, away from other patients and I was very well treated. I realised the staff were concerned about my condition, though I felt so ill at times that I really didn't care if I recovered or not. It was a strange feeling and I missed my children so much, but I knew it was safer for them not to visit until the virus was identified - it never was!

I understood that there were six of us, across the province of Ulster, who had contracted this mysterious virus. Out of the six, only myself, and one other person survived.

During my time in hospital, my temperature kept fluctuating. One night, as I lay in bed in the single room, I distinctly heard a bang on my window. I didn't really think much about it as I thought it was someone outside the window. However, this was impossible, because I later discovered that I was on the second floor of the hospital. A voice said: "You will soon be well again and home with your children."

I couldn't say if the voice was male or female.

The next morning, my temperature came back to normal and all my symptoms disappeared. Five days later, I was discharged from hospital and allowed to return home to my husband and children. In the three weeks that I had been unwell I had lost over two stone of weight and was very weak. It took me one full year to fully recover.

However, my illness put things into perspective. I realised I was extremely lucky to be alive. I also knew that, no matter what, my health was more important than anything else in this world, and I had our children to think about. My husband and I decided that I should take a step back from the family business. During this time we also had to cancel all our music gigs, but I wasn't sorry. Of course we missed the extra money, but it meant we had more time to spend together as a family.

In the months following this mysterious illness, most of the horrible premonitions were starting to fade. Instead, I was seeing more and more Angels. I was also receiving visits from some of my relatives who had passed on.

*

In 1981 I had another traumatic vision. By this time our boys were in their teens. Our oldest child, Peter, had passed his driving test. He had got himself a car and, like most boys of his age, he loved putting his driving skills to the test.

Peter and his younger brother, Kevin, had made plans to go out on the Saturday evening. That afternoon, I was standing at the sink washing the dishes, and, for a moment I had a vision of my son's car plunging down a steep embankment, rolling over and over, until it hit a large tree.

I knew that this was a warning sign from the Angels and I couldn't ignore it. I was so frightened. If I let our sons go out that evening without telling them what I had seen, they might never come home again. I didn't give Peter any details of the vision, but I told him I didn't think he needed to go out on that frosty night. I pleaded with him to stay at home but he refused to listen. He just said: "Mum, I have plans already made and I've promised two of my friends a lift to the disco." My heart almost stopped. I tried again to change his mind, but he wouldn't take any heed.

When the time came for them to leave, I asked Peter, to come to my bedroom so that I could speak to him privately. Again, I begged him not to go. I told him I had a bad feeling, but he told me I was being paranoid. He left the room and I followed both our sons and their two friends out to the car. I was so desperate that I just blurted out that I had seen their car rolling down a steep embankment. Again, they laughed and said: "There you go, imagining things, and we won't be near an embankment." I was then told to go into the house and stop embarrassing them.

That evening, I couldn't settle myself. I kept

waiting on the phone to ring or to hear a knock at the door. I don't believe I ever prayed as much in my life, as I did that night, that they would both return home safely.

At 2 am our house phone rang and, sure enough, it was the news I had been dreading. Peter told me that he had crashed the car. It was a complete write-off but, thankfully, no one was hurt. My husband and I drove to the crash scene to bring them home and I was very distressed by what I saw - their car was totally unrecognisable. To this day, I don't how any of the boys survived that crash. All I do know is that God and the Angels had answered my prayers that evening.

The following morning, I said to Peter: "I thought you weren't going to be on a road which had an embankment?" He told me that another friend had asked him for a lift home and he couldn't leave him stranded. On the way home, his car had hit black ice and spun out of control. After rolling down a steep incline, their car crashed head-on into a tree. I thanked God and their Guardian Angels that they were all safe.

From that point on, my family began to take my dreams and visions more seriously.

*

One sunny day in July 1985, I visited our local church during the weekly Eucharistic Adoration. On the altar, rows of candles were perfectly positioned on each side of the Blessed Sacrament. As I knelt down to pray, it seemed as though I was suspended in another time. It's difficult to explain, but it was as if the altar itself opened out to me. I had an inner sense of knowing, and vision, that beyond the altar was heaven. A feeling of pure ecstasy and peacefulness washed over me. It was a deep, spiritual experience, much too precious to describe.

It was during this remarkable vision, that I heard the same voice as I had heard in the hospital in 1978. The voice said to me: "Someone you love very much is going to come home, but I want you to know that, no matter what, I am with you always, to the end of time." Somehow, this message didn't seem to disturb me at the time. The voice was so reassuring that I was filled with a sense of calmness. Two hours later, I emerged from the church, although it seemed to me, I had only been there for a brief moment. I felt as if I had returned to Earth from another dimension. When I went outside to go home, it dawned on me, that something very special had happened. I went back into the church, but, of course, this divine vision of heaven was gone. The altar looked, as it looked on any day. I rushed home and told my husband: "You know, there really is a

God!" He looked puzzled and said: "I know."

A few months later, in September, my beloved mother passed away, the woman who, along with Archangel Raphael, had rescued me from the orphanage.

A chance remark from a friend, after my mum's funeral, reminded me of something mum had told me in June of that year. She was sick with a heavy cold and I had called down with some dinner on a Sunday afternoon. Whilst eating it, she told me that she had a visitor earlier that morning. I thought it had been one of her neighbours who had called, but I was very wrong. My mother told me that she had received a visit from her own mother, who had been dead for many years. Her mother had told her that she was: "Coming home soon." Even though I was a grown woman and had children of my own, I didn't want to think about my own mother passing on. It was upsetting to think of what life would be like without her. I told my mum I didn't want to know what my grandmother had come to tell her. My reaction didn't stop her and she told me anyway. I told her I didn't believe her. After all the times that I had been told by my parents and my husband that what I had seen or heard was 'only a dream,' I found myself repeating these same words to my mother.

The truth was, that I didn't want to hear it. I just didn't want to lose her. My mother described her vision as the room lighting up with a very bright light and, out of the hazy mist, her mother whispered to her: "When the autumn leaves are falling, you will be coming home." As she was speaking, we both witnessed a beautiful, misty, white light all around her bedroom. We were both astounded at what had just happened, but, somehow, my mum found the strength inside to say: "Didn't I tell you?" I dismissed the message we both had received, even though I knew it was true and could not be ignored. I just couldn't bear the thought of my mother leaving me.

My mother was a true lady, who always faced the trials of life with such courage and grace. When the time came, she faced death with those same admirable qualities.

After the funeral, I found it very difficult, as we all do, when we lose someone close. On many occasions afterwards, I felt her presence around me but, somehow, I couldn't be consoled. I desperately missed her.

Dealing with the loss of a loved one is never easy. Perhaps, it is only when a parent or guardian passes over, that the finality of bereavement is fully brought home to us.

Naturally, growing up I depended on my parents, particularly my mother, for guidance and support. When she was called back home, I struggled to overcome the great sense of loss that I felt. For a period of my life, I was completely at a loss. The woman, who I had always relied on, was gone. In time, though, those painful wounds did heal and yours will too.

We may never truly accept the reason why someone so close to us has to die. We are all different. For some it may take months, even years, before they finally accept that their loved one has returned home, but it is important to remember that God and his Angels are always there to help, comfort and guide us through.

On a beautiful, Saturday morning in June 1986, my husband and I decided that we would go fishing. We knew that our trip wasn't going to be very successful, because there had been no rain and the water was very low in the river, but we thought we would give it a try, as we needed a break. Realising there wasn't much chance of catching anything, I contented myself with putting on bait and sitting down on the river bank, hoping a fish would take it. My husband moved on down the river to deeper water and I sat there enjoying the summer sun. The gentle flow of the river below was incredibly soothing and comforting. I soon forgot about my fishing rod and my intention to catch fish, as my mind began to wander. All of a sudden, my thoughts were interrupted, by what seemed to be my mother's voice behind me. She warned me not to go near the river. This didn't make any sense to me; after all I wasn't near the river. I was sitting high up on the river bank. A few minutes later her voice came again, this time a little sharper: "Don't go near the river!"

By now, I was quite perturbed, but I decided to ignore the voice and I certainly did not look behind me. Then her voice got louder and she said: "Whatever you do, do not go near the river!" By now, I was very scared. I jumped up and looked around me but, of course, my mum was nowhere to be seen. I shouted for my husband who came running, as he thought I was in trouble. When he reached me, he remarked on how pale I looked. I told him of my mother's warning, but I knew, by the way he looked at me, that he was growing concerned regarding my mental state, such a short time after my mother's passing. He insisted that we pack up our belongings and leave to go home. I was annoyed as we gathered up our fishing equipment, not because we were leaving to go home, but, because once again, as on many previous occasions, I was not being believed.

We started off for home and, as we made our way back up the river, we met a neighbouring fisherman, a good friend of ours. He decided that there was no better opportunity than now, for me to learn to fly-fish. He set about getting the fishing rod rigged up for me. His enthusiasm soon melted away my irritation and I agreed to give fly-fishing a try. Once he had the rod prepared, he proceeded to advise me to wade out into the middle of the river, which I did, but being a learner comes with its own disadvantages. It wasn't long before my line got snagged on the tree behind me. I had to come in closer to the bank to allow him to release the bait. He was urging me to go back to the spot where I had been standing, but, suddenly, I noticed a change in the river. The water seemed to be rising, which was very strange owing to the fact that there had been no rain for days.

Something told me things were not right. I shouted to my husband that something terribly strange was happening. As I was standing on a corner, I had no idea what was happening behind me. My husband and friend, on the other hand, were standing on a high bank and had a perfect view of what was going on up the river. They both urged me to come back closer to the bank but, because I was laden down with chest waders and fishing gear, and with the water steadily rising, I struggled to reach the bank. They both reached down to rescue me, but the speed and force of the water was almost too much. I was also worried that, because of their position, I would pull them both in. I told them to let me go. My thought, at that moment was that our family needed at least one parent. However, the men were having none of it, and, after quite a struggle, they managed to pull me out. We were all very badly shaken by this ordeal. Our friend told us he had fished that river for over fifty years and he had never experienced what was called a 'flash flood.' We heard afterwards that a spout had burst on the mountain.

As we walked through the field to our car, I silently thanked God, my Guardian Angel and my mother for saving my life. At that point, I realised my mother, whilst in heaven, was still around, keeping an eye on us all. It was a very comforting thought, and it also helped me to come to terms with her loss.

8
MEDJUGORJE

Quite by accident, in 1986, I heard Jesus' mother Mary was appearing on Earth, in a place called Medjugorje. I thought it was wonderful that Mary was appearing somewhere, whilst I was living on the Earth and I decided that I really needed to go there.

My husband and I talked it over and he urged me to go. I wished he could have come with me, but, with work commitments, it just wasn't possible. Little did I know it was to be the most memorable pilgrimage of my life.

I made enquiries and joined a group of fellow pilgrims from all over Northern Ireland, but the bonus was that two of the pilgrims on the trip were from my home town.

We arrived in to a military airport in Yugoslavia on a Tuesday evening, in a hot scorching sun. We travelled by bus to a small hamlet in the mountains. To say it was an experience, travelling along that narrow mountain road is indeed an understatement. However, we all arrived safely. At that time, the village was quite primitive and very serene. It was a refreshing change from the hustle and bustle of our own country. We learned there were no hotels or, indeed, any grandeur, which of course added to its quaintness. The people of the village opened their doors to us and we were treated almost as one of their family. What I noticed was, not only their hospitality, but the deep spirituality that everyone in the village seemed to have. Even though there appeared to be quite a lot of poverty, the local people were very humble and shared all they had with the pilgrims. One almost envied them; they were at peace with themselves. On the surface we had so much more, and yet I knew they had it all, not materialistic, worldly goods, but they were very wealthy, in God. For me, it was a wake-up call. If I was to find true peace of mind and happiness, I would have to look within, rather than outside, for stimulation.

The following morning, after our arrival, we set off for what everyone called the 'Big Mountain' and, indeed, that's exactly what it was. You needed to be fit to climb it. Our journey up to the top was a prayerful journey. It was so uplifting and enriching, and I absolutely loved it. Perhaps, it was the quietness of the whole area that made the experience so special. The only sound was the quiet murmurs of our prayers. As a group, who did not know one another, we really bonded together through the medium of prayer. On reaching the top of the mountain, we separated and everyone seemed to want to be alone. Well, I certainly did. With the silence all around us, it was easy to pray the prayer of the quiet and it was hugely rewarding. One could say I had discovered "food for my soul." We stayed up there for a long time, just enjoying the peacefulness of the Holy place. On the way back down, we prayed together again. We continued on our pilgrimage throughout the rest of the week, and it was during that time, that I spent quite a lot of time in quiet contemplation. In doing so, I met many inspirational people, who, like myself, were searching for something deeper - to connect with God.

On the Sunday before we were due to return home, a lady, whom I had met, asked me if I would accompany her up the mountain. I agreed. However, it would have been easier if we had gone immediately after breakfast, because it was noon when we left and it was extremely hot. Back then, there were no shops, so I filled a bottle with water before we left the house.

My new-found friend, because of the heat and the steepness of the mountain, was having difficulty. As we were navigating across a rock-strewn surface, I wasn't able to help her that much because I was trying to keep my own balance. Halfway up the mountain the lady tripped and fell. I bent down to help her up, and, in doing so, my sunglasses fell off. I happened to look up at the sky and, as long as I live, I will never forget what I saw. There, before me, was a massive, dazzling, bright apparition of Padre Pio. He looked so serene and peaceful and seemed to take up the whole of the sky. There was an amazing blue and white light surrounding him and I could feel a Godly healing energy emanate from him, across the whole of the land. Although he was not smiling, he appeared to have an inner smile, and I had a knowingness that he was telling me that, with God's help, everything on Earth could be managed.

I don't know how long I stood there, staring up at him, before my vision was interrupted by my friend's call for help, but it seemed only a few moments. I immediately went to her aid, but by the time I reached her, she had managed to get up on her feet. I looked up, but the vision was gone. My friend asked me how I could look at the sun without sunglasses. I didn't say why. It seemed inappropriate to mention it because, obviously, she had not seen the glorious sight that I had been so lucky to see.

We proceeded to the top of the mountain, and, when we eventually reached the top, the lady decided to rest and pray. I walked over to the Holy cross, and, as I knelt down to pray, what happened next was, in a sense, similar to what had happened to me, in my own church, in 1985. It seemed like the heavens opened, and I was suspended in a different time zone. The most radiant, beautiful lady appeared before me. I knew it was the mother of Jesus, but certainly not Our Lady of Medjugorje. She had three beautiful roses, across her chest, in gold, red and white and appeared to be wearing some sort of very pale, cream robe/gown. Her hair, which was flowing around her shoulders, appeared to be a darkish brown, and her feet were slightly suspended above the ground. When she spoke to me she was smiling and warm. What she told me was a personal message about my future life.

One of the things she said was that I would have a very difficult task ahead of me, but, with my strong faith, I would cope, because God had plans for me. Some of the revelations Mary made to me should have been extremely upsetting, but, somehow, like back in 1985, I knew everything would be alright. This I cannot explain. All I can say, is that there is no earthly explanation for how I felt. Just before the vision ended, this heavenly lady, who did not identify herself by name, said: "I am Jesus' mother." I assumed she was, somehow, connected to the roses. Then she finished off by saying: "Before you leave here I will send you a sign, and when you receive it, you will understand my visit to you." It was at this point my friend touched my shoulder and asked if I was alright. She told me that I had been in the same position for a long time, yet it seemed like only moments to me.

It took me a little while to realise where I was, again, it's too difficult to explain. At that moment I felt I had wings on my feet, and I did something I would never normally do. I took off down that mountain at great speed. I felt I was flying, but, of course I wasn't. When I reached the bottom of the mountain, and steadied up, I remembered I had left my friend to come down alone. I just sat there thinking about what I had witnessed. I felt truly ecstatic! Later that evening, my friend asked me what had happened. I didn't tell her. Somehow, I couldn't, it was too precious, and personal to share.

That night as usual, after dinner, we all prepared

to go to St. Peter's Church, but I decided at the last minute not to go. I believe I just wanted to be alone to think over what had happened.

The next morning, as we all sat down to breakfast, I listened to them making plans for that day, which was our last day in Medjugorje. I knew in my heart, that I would not be joining them. I wanted to spend my last day by myself, praying and thinking about the amazing and uplifting experiences I had and what I had been told. I pondered a lot on what the task Mary mentioned was to be, and, indeed, a few years later, I certainly understood.

Now, at that time, there were many stall-holders dotted around the village, but there was also a very small shop which sold little bits and pieces, mostly relating to Our Lady of Medjugorje and the apparitions. I had tried, on many occasions, to get into the shop but was unsuccessful, but I decided, as I set out that morning, to give it one last try. As I approached the shop, I observed that a lengthy queue had formed outside it. My initial thought was that I was out of luck once again. However, I stayed on in the hope that I might manage to get in, and I did. It was very hot as I was queuing, so I leaned up against a small wall. I was fanning myself down when there seemed to be some sort of commotion behind me. However, there were two very tall people blocking my view, so I couldn't quite see what was happening. The disruption continued for a few minutes. Then the crowd seemed to disperse, and, suddenly, this little old lady, who had managed to push her way through the crowd, was reaching to me, what appeared to be, a sheet of white paper.

Several of the people thought it was for them and reached out to grab it, but she was very determined to give to me. I accepted it and I was speechless when I turned it over, to find it was a picture of Our Lady, the one whom I had seen on the mountain!

To say I was flabbergasted would be an understatement. Then it dawned on me - this was the sign Mary had promised me. No words could describe how I felt. Getting into the shop seemed unimportant now. However, I did get in and I bought a few things to take home to my family.

As we prepared to leave the next morning, I looked around that Holy place, and I vowed I would return sometime before I died and I did. My second pilgrimage to Medjugorje was very different. I spent quite a lot of time on my own and possibly, because of that, I found many people approached me. I made many friends, and because I had been there before, I was able to tell other pilgrims where to visit. It was a great trip and I enjoyed it immensely.

*

Two years after my first trip to Medjugorje, my husband and I were preparing to go on our usual Tuesday fishing trip, when a delivery van pulled up at the door.

My husband asked me to go to the door. Neither of us had been expecting anything, so I assumed that the delivery driver was lost and needed directions. Going to the door, I told the delivery man that I thought he was at the wrong house, but he read the name and address on the parcel and I told him that he was at the correct house. As I accepted the parcel, I was intrigued. I had no idea what it could be. I brought it in and, as I unwrapped the paper and opened the box, I gasped in amazement. Lo and behold, it was a beautiful statue of my Lady from the Medjugorje Mountain!

My husband asked me where it had come from and I told him I had absolutely no idea. It was at this time I learned that this was Our Lady of the Roses. The only information that the box contained was a letter addressed to me, which said: 'Free Gift.' At that time, I felt my life was taking me down a road I had not been down before. Once again, Mother Mary was, in her own way, making contact with me.

The picture of Our Lady, Mary of the Roses, which was given to Gwen in Medjugorje.

*

The following year, a friend asked me if I would go to Medjugorje with her. I told her I would love to join her but I would need to run it past my family first. I spoke to Francis and my sons and it was agreed I should go.

The pilgrimage was over the Easter vacation. When we arrived at the airport and standing in the queue, my friend remarked that there were two women who seemed to be staring at us. I hadn't noticed anything, but after a short time had passed, I began to notice these women were actually staring at us quite a lot. I didn't really attach any importance to them; after all I didn't know or recognise them. On board the plane, it was strange that these two women were actually seated beside us. We began chatting and I discovered that, like my friend, this was also their first trip to Medjugorje. These two ladies were very excited, and it wasn't long before we became friends. It was even stranger that, when we arrived at our destination, the four of us were allocated to the same house. We had an amazing week; we did the pilgrimage together and enjoyed it immensely.

The night before we were due to leave, the girls asked if I could come alone to their room later that evening. It seemed an odd request but I agreed I would go. When I arrived at the room, we talked a lot about our week spent together, and it became obvious that my two young friends were indeed very spiritual. They even told me how they had successfully managed to start up a prayer group in their home town. During our conversation, one of them said to the other: "Aren't you going to tell her?" What happened then, I can only describe as a bombshell being dropped on me. The story shook me, but I knew that they were speaking the truth.

One of the girls told me, that she was in her bedroom one morning when she had, what she believed was, a vision on her bedroom wall. In the vision a woman spoke to her about a situation in her life which included her friend. When my new friend had finished her story, she asked me to guess who the woman had been. Of course I mentioned Our Lady, her Guardian Angel, even her late mother, but no, she said it was me! "That is why we were staring at you in the airport, because I recognised you!" the girl told me.

It took me quite sometime to come to terms with this revelation. I had never encountered anything quite like this before. I had no idea where I could possibly fit into this. I kept in contact with the girls for a while, and the last I heard was that their prayer group was stronger than ever.

Over the years, I have visited many Holy places including Knock, Lough Derg and Lourdes. These special places have all been stepping stones on my Spiritual journey with God and the Angels.

9
FAITH AND HOPE IN ILLNESS

Life went on, and things were as they are in any family life. We were working and doing the usual things that families do. Then, in May 1989, my husband started to complain about being unwell. However, it was December, just before Christmas, when all the results came in as to what was ailing him.

After attending the hospital, he was contacted and asked to come back. It was a Friday and it had been snowing. Arriving at the hospital, my husband suggested that I should go to the café and wait for him. A little time passed and he came in and asked me to come with him. I was puzzled, but I accompanied him. We were just going out of the hospital door when he told me the news. He had been diagnosed with cancer. Everything in my life just seemed to standstill, as my mind registered what he had just said. We were both in shock. No words can explain the tremendous effect it had on both of us, and later, our family.

Francis needed treatment, but, with it being so

close to Christmas, it was decided he would go into hospital in the New Year. An operation was scheduled and it proved to be a successful one. These were very dark days for our family.

On the night after the operation, I was sitting with my husband when he told me that the procedure was very successful; all the cancer had been removed. This was a special time for us. The dark cloud had been lifted. My family and I, along with my husband's family, were delighted with the result.

However, later in the week, the nurse, in charge of the Intensive Care Unit, approached me and asked me to meet with the surgeon the following morning. Intuitively, I knew something was wrong so I asked our eldest son, Peter, to accompany me. We both were suspicious about a doctor wanting to speak with us over the weekend, but we kept our spirits up in the hope that all was well. The following morning, the surgeon told us they had tested the tumour and what he believed, was confirmed. It was malignant. I said to him: "My husband told me he thought you had taken it all away," but the surgeon said that he had removed most of it, but didn't get it all. He told us the cancer would come back.

We reeled at this news; we had all been on a high. It was sometime before we went back into the ward. Our youngest son of ten years old was there with his dad, so it was important we didn't tell him this news. It was apparent, over the next three years that my husband was totally unaware of the doctor's findings. Peter and I kept the news to ourselves. We thought it best that everything returned to normal for our family. It was a tough three years for our son, Peter, and myself. We carried on the family business and eventually my husband was well enough to take over the running of it again.

Almost to the day the doctor had predicted, my husband became unwell again and, on New Year's Eve, another operation was scheduled. We were told it would be the evening before my husband would be returned back to the ward, so we were told to wait until after 6 pm to ring. We prayed all day and there seemed to be no reason to get worried. After all, the last operation had gone very well. It was around 3.30 pm when the hospital called. The nurse asked me if I was alone. I told her that our second son, Kevin, was with me. She asked if we could come to the hospital immediately. We were very worried. On arriving at the hospital, I could see that my husband was very upset. He told us the surgeon wasn't able to do anything. We were devastated. I don't believe we ever prayed as much for guidance, to help soften the blow my husband had suffered at this news, and our prayers were answered.

In consultation later, the doctor said: "There may be a way out of this." He would contact the Cancer Centre in Belfast and see if treatment was possible, and it was. Francis started his treatment just before Easter of that year. We travelled every day, Monday to Friday, for a month and, on Good Friday, at exactly 3 pm, he received his last treatment. On the journey home my husband remarked to me: "Did you notice I received my last treatment at 3 pm? That has to be a good sign from God." And indeed it was. Once again the sun started to shine for us.

*

When a loved one becomes ill, it can feel like a dark cloud has settled over the home. Waiting for a diagnosis to be made, can seem like a very long time of anxiety and fear, whilst always trying to remain positive, until finally you hear the news. When a serious illness is diagnosed, our worst fears are realised, not only for the patient, but also for the whole family circle.

There are endless visits to the doctor's surgery and to hospitals, in the hope that treatment will be available for the patient. You feel you have been taken into a world you have never known, a lost feeling, as you try to listen to the doctors and nurses explaining the situation to you. Being in shock most of the time, the information we hear does not always make sense.

From my experience with illness, I know and appreciate the encouragement and support I received from my family and friends. People tend to pull together in times of crisis.

Do not be afraid to accept their help and support. There's a time to give and a time to receive and in times of sickness, be open to accepting all the help and support offered.

We all settled down and things went reasonably smooth. It was apparent during this time, especially in the last two years, that we couldn't hold on to the business any longer. We knew something would have to be done if we were to get through. My husband and a close friend suggested that I go back to school. I started off by doing a simple word processing course, two mornings a week. I felt guilty at leaving my husband, but he always encouraged me to keep going. I sat a few exams and surprised myself by passing them with flying colours. It was then I realised just how low my confidence was.

It took a lot of courage to keep going. However, I did get a boost of confidence when I realised I could do this. I went on to study English and Psychology and finished up studying for a Counselling course. I have to say, it was during studying for the Counselling course, that I discovered I needed counselling myself, and that was a revelation. I furthered the line of Psychology by attending an Ennegram weekend, and, again, it was an eye opener as to who I really was. It took a long time for me to come to terms with how my life path was changing. For too long, I had hidden behind a mask. I now realised that this was the beginning of my Spiritual journey.

During this time, I picked up a few jobs and it was good therapy for me, to be out among people again. However, holding down a full-time job wasn't really working for us. There were many ups and downs with my husband's health and many trips to hospitals, and I didn't want to be anywhere else except to be available for him. He was an amazing patient and, when he was feeling well, we were up and away to pursue our hobbies. Many times during this period, I often asked myself where God and my Angels were. It seemed they had deserted me as I was having fewer and fewer experiences with them.

During this challenging time, my husband never lost faith. He was a deeply religious man. He prayed tirelessly, and never missed church. I went along with him, but at this time I believe I had hit a dry period on my Spiritual journey.

It was at this time, in July of 1996, that I was working in the garden. On turning around, I had a vision of my mother. She was standing there before me. She spoke to me and said: "Stop worrying. Everything will be alright and all is going according to God's plan." As quickly as she had appeared, she was gone!

I glanced over at our youngest son, Philip, who was also in the garden, to see if he had seen her too, but it was obvious he hadn't. He said: "Is there something going on over there?" I told him everything was fine, so obviously he had sensed something had happened, but I didn't tell him. I sat down on the step beside him and he asked me again:

"Was there something going on when you were over there, mum?" I said to him: "Why do you ask?" He said he didn't know; he just sensed something was happening. After my mother's visit, the Angels began to appear to me on a regular basis. I settled down and felt very happy. I took great comfort from them.

*

In November of that year, very suddenly, after a short illness, my brother Graham passed away. I felt a great loneliness at his loss. After the funeral, I stayed a few days with my sister-in-law. On a cold, December night, as we travelled home, I asked my husband: "Do you think my brother is in heaven?" He replied: "Of course he is."

Secretly, I asked God and the Angels to send me a sign. I think it was during our drive home that I got a chance to really think about what the loss of my brother meant to me. When we arrived home, on one of our rose bushes, was a single rose in bloom. I was shocked, owing to the fact that it was minus 4 degrees. I got the torch and looked into the centre of this rose and, difficult as this may be to believe, I actually saw my brother's face in the centre. I felt elated. I went to bed knowing my brother was in heaven. I thanked God for the revelation.

I thought a lot about my mother at that time, and how she had appeared to me a few months earlier to reassure me that all would be well. I now know she is close by, looking in on us, from time to time. She loved us in life and still loves us, even though we cannot always see her. It's good to know she is always close by, watching over and protecting us as we journey on life's mission.

10
A VEIL OF DARKNESS

It was the following year that I began to have a few 'down days.' Somehow, I was unable to snap out of it. I fought very hard, but to no avail. Slowly but surely, I slipped into a world of my own. Depression was not an illness I had ever thought I would suffer. Indeed, I had tried to help other people overcome these dark periods in their lives. Reflecting back on the times I had tried to be there for others, I realised I knew nothing about the illness. It's only when one experiences an illness themselves that they can fully comprehend how another person really feels.

Depression can be hidden from the victim for quite some time, and when they do realise what is happening, they try to conceal it. In today's society it is fast becoming an understood illness. For too long it has been looked upon as some sort of stigma. Perhaps that is why we try to hide it. For me, the illness was a long, lonely road, and one I travelled alone.

There were many corners to turn and, for me, each corner I came to, I believed, once again, I would see the light which would lead me into good mental health. Alas, that was not to be. Each day I sank deeper and deeper into a world of darkness from which I was unable to return.

My husband and family of five fantastic sons had no idea of the illness. During this time my husband was in remission and had quite good health. He did all he could, but I had to struggle with this by myself. I was so lonely and desolate.

For quite some time I wore the mask of: "Everything is fine." Eventually, I could no longer hide it. My days were spent going back to bed, lying in the darkness of our bedroom, and praying for a miracle. It was during this time my frustration with God and the Angels reared its nasty head on a daily basis. I believed my prayers were not being heard. I stopped going to Church, and having to go to the shops was a nightmare. I cut myself off completely from my friends. It was then my family realised things were getting out of hand. They rallied around, and tried to help me. This made me feel guilty at what I was putting them through, but I was powerless to help myself. My condition worsened. Many suggestions were made but I wasn't listening. I wanted to be left alone to suffer, in silence.

The highlight of my day was thinking about how much I was looking forward to meeting my mum and dad, my two brothers, not to mention my biological mother. It became like an addiction wanting to die; the question was how? At times I thought it would be unfair to my family. Then I would sink into the darkness again, and nothing seemed all that important. I fought very hard against those dark thoughts. At times I felt I was winning; other times, I just didn't care. I just wanted off planet Earth.

It was during one of my dark periods, as I was lying in bed one morning at about 11 am, that the bedroom lit up and there was Padre Pio! I just stared at him and he at me. Then a voice spoke and said: "Come, my child, you have much to do." Then he was gone. At that time I wondered: "Did I imagine that?" But I knew I hadn't. I lay on in bed thinking about it and I felt a little better. I managed to get dressed that day. However, I didn't really feel up to doing anything else. A few days went by and for the first time in two and a half years, I decided to try and go for a walk. I left the house and chose a road I knew where I would be unlikely to meet anyone. I still felt too vulnerable. Little did I ever imagine that I would have a second meeting, so soon, with Padre Pio! I had walked for about a quarter of a mile, when, out of nowhere, he joined me. I asked him to help me and his response was: "This illness of yours is God's plan for you my child." With that he was gone. I can remember thinking at the time: "Well, no harm to God, I really don't want this illness!"

From that point on, I had more good days than bad. On the days I was feeling low, I was really low. On the good days, I dwelt too much on the 'tomorrow.' Questions tormented me like: "What if this never goes away?" or "What if I never manage to shake off these dark thoughts?"

My family urged me to seek medical advice, but I was having none of that. Then a lifelong friend came on the scene. She immediately knew I was not the person she had always known. I made many excuses for not wanting to see her, but she persevered. Eventually, with my family and friend's encouragement, and much persuasion, I went to my local surgery, which I just about got the courage to do. My doctor acted promptly, and, within three days I had a two-hour appointment with a psychiatrist. He immediately advised medication and counselling, which I was reluctant to accept. The treatment started almost at once, and he reassured me I would return to full health.

At that time, I began to realise I was not alone. My family, my many good friends, and the local doctors were all there for me. The miracle was not instantaneous but, very slowly, I began to see a small light of hope.

It was during this recovery period, that a friend invited me to go to a nearby town where a group met regularly, whose members were suffering from the same illness. I received a warm welcome from everyone there. My gratitude for that group has never been forgotten. I attended the meetings regularly and made a lot of new friends, and those friendships remain strong to this day.

It was during this time, on a cold, bleak December morning, I found myself sitting at a lake which was close to our home. How I got there, I have no idea, yet I know I travelled there in our car. I sat there looking at the water, thinking about how I felt and wondering where it had all gone wrong. All of a sudden, this big, burly man, dressed in his full fishing gear, chest waders, wet coat and a hat, was standing before me. I'd say he was in his early forties. He sat down on the bench beside me and I noticed that he also had a fishing rod. He spoke to me and asked me if I did any fishing. Before I knew it, I was telling him about all the fishing trips I had with my husband and all the fish we had caught. I didn't ask him his name, or where he was from, nor did he ask me. It was difficult for me to chat because, over the previous few years, I had tried to avoid all contact with people. After about fifteen or twenty minutes he said: "Gwen, perhaps it's time for you to go home now." I was stunned by the fact that he knew my name. He got up from the bench and he patted me on the shoulder. His last words were: "Gwen, God be with you."

I watched him go, but then I decided to follow him and ask who he was, but he was gone! I walked back towards my car, but this mystery man was nowhere to be seen. I stood there, and looked around the bleak place where I was and wondered what I was doing there.

When I arrived back home, I told my husband I had been speaking to a fisherman at the nearby lake. He looked puzzled and said: "Well, I don't know who you were speaking to, but he was not fishing. The fishing season is over and will not reopen until

April."

This gave me food for thought. It was a long time later that I realised that the man, whom I had been talking to, was not of this world!

*

Life went on, and things got better for me. I was able to go out and about, and Francis and I took up our hobby of fishing again. I also got into the habit of taking our dogs out for a walk every morning, to a lovely spot near our home, which I frequently visited. While I was there, I let the dogs off their leads and they ran free. I rarely saw anyone, just the odd car passing. However, there was one farmer, who tended his sheep in the area and he would have been there quite often. This gentleman was friendly with an old lady whom I knew very well. One day I got a phone call from this particular lady. She asked me to come and see her. When I did, she asked me who the young fellow was that was out walking with me the previous day. I told her there was no one with me except the dogs. She said that her farmer friend had seen me with a young man who was over eight foot tall and was 'not of this world.' I laughed and told her that perhaps her friend was suffering from delusions, but she kept insisting that this gentleman had seen him. She told me that he had got such a fright, and, indeed, thinking it over, this farmer was not easily frightened! I told my husband about it and his answer was as usual: "I wish I could see what he had seen." On the strength of this I accepted the story and truth be told, I felt good that someone had actually witnessed this heavenly being, whom I believe, was protecting me from any imminent danger, and working for my higher good. This gentleman had the privilege of seeing this beautiful being, who I now believe was Ray, my Guardian Angel. We know that everyone has Guardian Angels that accompany them and protect them on their journeys throughout their lives.

*

Depression has now been recognised as a serious illness which affects one in every four people in their lifetime. Medical science has made a major breakthrough by developing a scan which is being used to show, in the patient's brain, how when one is ill, the brain can only send negative thoughts. This scan is not only helpful to the patient, but also to the patient's doctor in deciding which form of treatment is most effective.

Guidance for sufferers:
When you realise that you are suffering from depression, seek medical help immediately.
Do not wait until you are in that dark hole and unable to climb out of it. Trying to mask it from family and friends is a mistake.
Try to be courageous and ask for the help you need. Remember you are stronger than the depression and are worthy of living a healthful life for yourself.

Guidance for family and friends:
If you have a family member, or friend, who confides in you that they are suffering from

depression, don't try to make light of their illness. After all, if they told you they had a serious, physical illness, you wouldn't brush it off lightly. In the beginning, encourage the patient to take baby steps.

Don't force them to do anything they don't wish to do. Too much, all at once, may prove to be overwhelming.

The most important thing you can do is let your loved one know that you are there for them, because time is the greatest gift you can give to anyone.

**Hope and prayer soar up high
Building bridges in the sky.**
(Grainne Keogh- Kelly)

11
A NEW DAWN

In time, my mental health was fully restored. One day, just out of the blue, a mutual acquaintance asked me if I would like to go to an Angel workshop. I replied: "How can you have an Angel workshop?" She told me to come along and find out for myself, which I did. I was only in the room about thirty minutes, when I realised that I had, at last, discovered what I had been searching for my whole life. Everything was beginning to make sense. There were so many people present, that I could identify with. I was so pleased. I was not alone in my experience of visions of auras, Angels etc. I kept very quiet and listened to other people's stories, about how they had seen Angels. From that point on, I researched every aspect of the phenomena I had experienced all my life.

After that, my life changed dramatically. My headaches cleared completely and, perhaps, for the first time in my life, I felt it was ok to be me. The mask I had been wearing for so many years came off. My confidence improved immensely. I acquired the three stages of Reiki, a Holistic Healing modality, which I practised on my husband. He thoroughly enjoyed it, and said it brought him an amazing calmness.

Along with my friends, we started to discuss Angels. It was such a relief to be able to share some of my experiences, and, indeed, to hear of their experiences. I didn't feel the need to pretend anymore, about who I really was. My friends and I would meet regularly and have discussions about our Angelic experiences, sharing our stories and engaging in meditations.

One day, a life-long, close friend asked me if I would consider speaking openly about my experiences with the Angels. She also suggested that maybe some day it would even encourage me to write a book. I agreed, and almost immediately, I had misgivings. After all, I was not a public speaker! I wondered how I was ever going to manage.

A few days later, Francis and I were fishing at the Moyola River, when this radiant, heavenly being appeared to me. He said: "I am Ray, your Guardian Angel. You remember we used to play together?" In that moment, all my childhood memories of playing with Ray came flooding back. My mind was buzzing, because my Ray was a little girl, but this Angel, who stood before me, was a handsome, young man. He must have read my thoughts, because he smiled and, somehow, I was able to read his mind: "I can be anyone I want to be," he seemed to say.

Just then, a mass of white Angel feathers

showered down on me and my Guardian Angel. The sky lit up with beautiful, bright lights. Ray assured me that I could, and would, be able to share my experiences about the Angels with others, and, perhaps, one day, write a book about my experiences. At that time, I never could have visualised myself writing a book, but it has now come to pass. Ray said: "You will spread the word about Angels." He assured me that God and his helpers would be there to aid me every step of the way. Then, just like Our Lady in Medjugorje, he told me he would send me a sign.

A few weeks later, a meeting was arranged with like-minded friends, who were eager to learn more about their Guardian Angels. As the date approached, the more apprehensive I became. A short time later, a friend of mine, who knew nothing about our gathering, arrived on our doorstep. She said to me: "I have no idea what I'm doing here and certainly no idea why I brought this for you!" She then handed me a little box. I opened it, and inside, was an Angel, and written on it was: "The Angels are here with you always." I knew instantly that this was the message from Ray.

The meeting was planned for a Saturday afternoon and only a few of my closest friends knew about it. However, before long, the phone started ringing with people asking if they could come along. We turned no one away. In the end, we had to run the meeting over two days.

The day of the first meeting arrived, and when I

saw so many people coming in our gate, I panicked. I said to my husband and son: "Oh what have I done? I can't do this!" But they both said the same thing: "Well, you're going to have to, because there is no one else in this house who can!" I ran down to the bedroom and begged my Angels for help. It was then that I saw Ray. He smiled at me and said: "I promised we would help you." At these words I felt so calm. I've no idea, to this day, how, but everything went very well. Everyone enjoyed the meeting so much and they asked me when we were going to arrange another one.

Slowly, our small group grew in size, with many more friends coming and learning to meditate with God and the Angels. It was beautiful to see everyone getting so much out of these gatherings.

It was at this time, shortly after the first Angel meeting, a young woman approached me, while I was out shopping, and asked me if she and two friends could join our prayer group. I told her we would contact her soon. Around this time, my husband's illness had flared up again and I wasn't quite sure what to do. I prayed very hard for guidance and, of course, my prayers were answered. I told both my husband and my friends about these three young women wanting to come. They agreed that bringing Angel energy could only bring positive power into our home. I contacted the lady and arranged a date for our Angel meeting. I don't think I will ever forget the sight of those young women on that cold, October night. When I opened the door, they stood there, like three little Angels. When I brought them in, the first thing I noticed, was a beautiful, white light, tinged with purple, that surrounded each of them. They were so excited and looking forward to learning about the Angels. That night went extremely well.

I suppose you could say that, as well as the Angel gatherings, spiritual healing was taking place for all who showed an interest in God and the Angels. Those three young women were the first of a long stream of people who wanted to spend time meditating and being in the company of God and the Angels. The girls decided to keep a journal of any Angel experiences they had, which has proved to be a very enlightening idea.

Indeed, one could say the Angels have been very busy inspiring us all to call upon them during our walk with God. Over the years, I have seen and heard of many occurrences where spiritual beings have returned to protect us.

In Chapter 13 of this book, "Stories of Hope," there is an outline of some of these Angelic encounters. It is hoped that these stories will inspire many more people, who are eager to learn about Angels, as they journey through life, completing their Godly mission, before returning to their eternal home.

12
BEREAVEMENT

It was in 2008 that things began to change quite rapidly with regards to my husband, Francis' health. After almost twenty years of prayer and medical assistance, it appeared the drugs were not quite as effective as they had been in the previous years of treatment of his illness. For the first time, he began to have a lot of pain and sleepless nights. Many visits were made to his doctor and his oncologist and, after much discussion, it was decided to try and treat the pain with another form of chemotherapy. Unfortunately, Francis had a severe reaction to this new drug and it had to be stopped immediately. It was then that his consultant decided that another operation was a possibility.

On Holy Thursday of that year, an operation was carried out, one which saved his life, as he had been deteriorating rapidly for some time. When Francis came home from hospital, his convalescence was very slow and not without its setbacks. However, Francis recovered quite well and, in September of that year he was able to return to what can be described as a 'normal life'. In the months following the operation, whilst he was 'out of the woods' regarding his illness, it was obvious things were not the same as they had been. However, we carried on with our lives as usual, as best we could.

In the Spring of 2009, Francis returned to his favourite hobby of fishing. Here, he seemed to find solace and peace in the quietness surrounding the Moyola River and, as always, he was overjoyed at bringing home the brown trout for evening tea. For many years, we walked with our dogs on some of the most beautiful, scenic routes around our home, but we would always return to our favourite haunt by the Moyola River, and stroll around in this lovely place of stillness and beauty. As always, on arriving at the fast flowing river, we sat with a picnic, watching the dogs play in the water. We both knew, in our hearts, that these were precious moments which we spent together.

 As a family, we spent as much time together, as possible. We had barbecues, trips to Donegal and visits to our extended families, and we often had our grandchildren stay over with us. Life was good, and during this time God blessed us with our first great-grandchild, a boy. However, as the New Year of 2010 approached, we realised that the illness was rampant again. We visited the oncologist, who advised us that there was no more treatment available. In June of the same year, Francis was admitted to hospital for respite for one month. Somehow, after that, things started to go downhill. He was still able to do a little fishing, which he enjoyed, and on many occasions, he played the trumpet and listened to his favourite jazz music. Francis was a wonderful patient, who never, ever complained, yet it was obvious that he was suffering. His last fishing trip was to Bundoran, to fish in the River Drowse. Whilst there, we spent a lovely weekend with our friends, Angela and Kenny, who also loved fishing. As I watched Francis fish with such energy, over that weekend, I wondered if the doctor's diagnosis was correct. It was a holiday I will always remember, as our friends did everything possible to ensure we both enjoyed our trip. Kenny saw to all our needs regarding the fishing, and Angela packed an amazing picnic hamper for us to enjoy on the river-bank. When we came in from our fishing trip, dinner was served immediately. We returned home on the 15th August, our son, Philip's, birthday. We, somehow, knew that this was the last trip we would have together. From that time, until God called a beloved husband and precious father home, we spent every day together.

It was the 16th August, and I had just returned from shopping. When entering our home, I called out to Francis, but there was no answer. I searched around for him and discovered he was in the room in our home where we had our prayer meetings. He appeared to be sleeping. I quietly sat down beside him. Almost immediately, the room was filled with a beautiful, illuminating, white light. I was very excited as I had seen this light before, and I knew it heralded the entrance of a heavenly being. And it did! The most beautiful, young Angel stood before us. She had long, blonde hair and her countenance was beyond description. She looked at us lovingly, and then I noticed my beloved father standing at her right hand side. Daddy looked as he had always looked, though much younger than when he had passed away. He did not communicate with me. However, this striking, young Angel did. In a soft voice she said: "My name is Rachael, and I am one of your Guardian Angels. I am here to comfort you and to protect you." I was confused as to whether this was Ray, the playmate I had when I was a child. She must have known my thoughts, because she assured me that she was, indeed, a new Guardian Angel, who had come to be with me. She also told me that the people on Earth have many Guardian Angels. Then, they both were gone. I turned to Francis, but refrained from mentioning my vision to him. However, he was very excited about his own vision! He told me he did not know if he was dreaming or not, but in the vision he was at the Last Supper with Jesus and the apostles. He said he was helping to serve out the food to them, going around the tables, and he was feeling very honoured to be serving Jesus.

Afterwards, I pondered over both our visions and wondered what they might mean.

It was the 29th August and, for the first time in almost twenty-two years, Francis went to bed for a rest during the afternoon. We called the doctor in and she told us to call all immediate relatives home, as time was getting short. On the 4th September, in the early morning, surrounded by his family, Francis quietly left this Earth and went home to God. Even though we thought we were well prepared for his leaving, no words can describe the aftermath of shock, despair and loneliness. The only way I survived this loneliness, was with the love and support I received from my sons and their families, from my extended family and my niece Kathleen, who stayed with me as often as she could, even though she was still grieving for her dad, who had passed over two years previously. Also the support from my many friends, who helped me to accept that my life-journey still had to go on and that I had a very important role to play as a mother, a grandmother and friend. I suppose, I could say, we helped each other, because I knew we were all grieving for someone we loved so much.

*

A few months after Francis had passed over, my friend, Angela, asked me if I would like to help her by minding her children whilst she was at work. I jumped at the chance and said: "Yes!" I believed this would help get me out of bed in the mornings, instead of lying on with my memories. Still, on the first morning, as I drove to her house, my thought was: "I cannot do this!" I felt like turning and going back home. However, I continued on to Angela's home. When I arrived, there were three wee faces looking out of the window and they looked so excited to see me. I was very glad I hadn't turned back and gone home. From the moment I walked into Angela's home, I never got a minute to think about my own troubles. Spending time with Angela's children was the best therapy I could ever have had. They knew nothing about grief and they expected me to be my usual self with them. We played cards, hide-and-seek, went for walks etc. I will always be grateful to Angela, Kenny and their children, for helping me so much during one of the most traumatic periods of my life. At that time, my grandchildren were not living in Draperstown, so it was only at the weekends that I spent precious time with them, too. I had the best of both worlds with all the children.

Time went on and, with great encouragement from family and friends, I eventually returned to my prayer meetings, and leading meditations, with many like-minded people. My wonderful encounters with the Angels and the divine realm continued, as they do to this day.

*

The loss of a child is a devastating loss for any parent. The bond between mother and baby begins when the baby is in the womb and continues through life and that bond does not diminish as the child grows older. We do not expect to outlive our children, and yet, in December 2015, I realised that was exactly what was happening.

On the 22nd November 2015, Kevin, my second son, and I were travelling home, having spent a few days together in Donegal. We talked about our future plans and we discussed the possibility of visiting Barcelona the following spring-time. We had both already visited the city on our own, but this time, we decided to travel together, to see the sights once more. As we enjoyed making these plans, little did I know that, instead of going to Barcelona with Kevin, I would be attending his funeral in just two weeks from that day.

On the 2nd December 2015, Kevin's health suddenly began to fail rapidly and he was immediately admitted to hospital and into the Intensive Care Unit. Two days later, on the 4th December, my son was called home to God. Within a few days, I had experienced a rollercoaster of feelings, from the joyful prospect of holidaying together, to the disbelief, shock and despair of my son's death. The shock was paramount, not only for me to lose a precious son, but also for my other four sons to lose a beloved brother. Winter had set in outside, and I felt it had settled in our hearts and homes as well.

The loss of a child of any age is overwhelming but, in time, the pain ceases to be as constant, and with each and every day thereafter, God and the Angels give you strength to try and help you to understand why a child was taken home before their parent. There are no answers to this. I had so much help from family and friends, who comforted and supported me, in my efforts to cope with this great loss. Each day brings different memories, some to make you smile and others to grip at your heart. Now, as difficult as it is to look at those special photos of my child, it brings back so many happy memories of the time we have had together. With my deep faith in God, I believe that everything is in divine timing and God's plan for Kevin was to bring him home sooner than I would have wished. However, this does not alleviate the great loss I feel in my heart.

I will always cherish the happy times we shared together as a whole family. I am comforted by these memories and with the knowledge that Kevin is reunited with his daddy, Francis, in heaven.

There is no easy way to cope with the loss of a child, whether the child is a youngster or an adult. In our own way, each of us cope with it the best we can. It really helps to always accept any comfort and support offered from family and friends.

Each and every one of us loses someone close to us, at some time during our lifetime on Earth. Grief is a very profound and personal journey with which we must reconcile ourselves, in our attempts to go on with our lives, as best we can. Without our loved one, many emotions rise within us: shock, anger, guilt, broken-heartedness etc. When we feel we just cannot go on living without them, three coping strategies can surface: fight, flight or freeze.

For me, I froze, and owing to this traumatic reaction, I have found that my memory of certain events, surrounding the loss of my husband and son, has completely vanished.

Behind every smile, there can be a million unshed tears, but I just learned to cope, and accept the abundance of love and support, showered on me by family and friends. But no one can ever fill the empty space that is left within our hearts.

However, as a result of a lifetime of divine encounters, I totally believe that our deceased loved ones are very happy and at peace, in a beautiful place, we call heaven. They are now released from the bonds of this physical dimension and are reunited with their loved ones. They are now totally free and are blissfully happy in the presence of God and the Angels.

13
STORIES OF HOPE

A Heavenly Being On The Mountain

One dry, Autumn evening, my son Philip and I were out for a walk on the mountain, close to our home. We had decided to take our dogs, Katie and Patty, with us. We were on our way back down the mountain, walking in the direction of our car, and, as always, I was hoping not to bump into any other walkers with dogs. As we walked along, we could scan the entire mountain path. It was unlikely that someone else could be on the mountain, without us seeing them. However, as we approached a small bridge, this small figure suddenly appeared from nowhere. As we drew nearer, I realised he was indeed quite a small man. I also noticed how ordinarily dressed this man was. My son and I stopped and spoke very briefly to him. We chatted about the weather and the beautiful, mountain scenery. Then the man said: "I have walked from a long way off." There was something about the way he spoke that struck a chord within me. I knew that he was in some way special. He then placed his hand on my shoulder and said to us: "God be with you both," before continuing on his walk.

As Philip and I walked away, we both remarked on how strange it had been that the man had just appeared out of nowhere. As we looked back up the steep mountain path, he was nowhere to be seen.

We were totally confused as to where he had gone. Philip ran back and even looked under the bridge, but the man had disappeared without a trace.

An Angel Escort Home

Another Angelic experience our son Philip had, was after a night out with his friends, when he encountered, what we believe, was his Guardian Angel manifesting himself, and showing Philip that he was there to protect him.

One Saturday night, Philip set out to go to Cookstown, a town approximately twelve miles from our hometown. It was in the middle of winter and it was a bitterly cold night. Despite my warnings to him to wear a coat, he left the house without one. I had told him, if he and his friends needed a lift home, to ring home. However, he reassured me that they had booked a taxi.

At around 2 am Philip arrived back home, later than usual. He seemed quite shaken and I was worried that something had happened. He told me he had got talking to old friends outside the bar and his taxi had left without him. He then set off walking towards home.

There are two roads home from Cookstown to Draperstown - one is shorter but is very dangerous, with a number of hairpin bends. Philip told me that he started to walk in the direction of the shorter road. He believed that if a car was to come along, most likely it would be travelling to Draperstown. Sure enough, a car pulled up and Philip, very willingly, got in. However, rather than drive straight on towards home, the car turned around and drove back in the direction of Cookstown.

Philip said there was very little conversation between him and the driver, which made him feel uneasy. Without telling him, somehow the driver knew exactly where Philip lived. He took him straight to the door. When Philip got out of the car, he looked back towards the driver and was shocked to see that the man was a mirror image of himself! As the car drove off, he realised that the car was the same colour and model as his own.

I assured him it was his Guardian Angel who had brought him safely home. He smiled and said: "Imagine, I have seen my Guardian Angel and he looks exactly like me!"

A White Light

While out working in Geneva, our son, Peter, fell very ill. He lay in an apartment for a few days before he realised how ill he was. Worried about him, his work colleagues took him to hospital. There was only one surgeon in the whole hospital that could speak English fluently. My son was very lucky that this surgeon happened to be on duty that day. Several tests were carried out, and it was discovered that Peter required immediate surgery.

In the days and weeks following the operation, Peter's surgeon visited him when he could, often bringing English newspapers and books for him to read.

During this time, Peter reflected on what he had experienced. All he remembered was being wheeled down the corridor as he lay on a hospital trolley. At some point he recalls being in a very dark place, in what he can only describe as a tunnel. He said he was travelling towards a bright, white light and the feelings of release, love and peacefulness that washed over him were like nothing he had ever experienced before. Then, all of a sudden, it went dark again. The day before he was to be discharged from hospital, his surgeon came to visit. It was the last time he would see him, and during their parting conversation, the surgeon told Peter that during his surgery, they had lost him for a few minutes.

To this day we can only conclude that this was a Near Death Experience (NDE).

An Army Of Angels

This is a story that I was told by a local lady when I was just in my teens. However, it is one that I have never forgotten.

In a parish in County Antrim, there was an ongoing dispute between local farmers. The dispute was concerning a land right-of-way. Most of the farmers had clubbed together, against a local man called Joe, who would not agree, or change his mind about giving access to the neighbouring farmers, to use the right-of-away. The disagreement had been ongoing for quite some time. Parties had played tricks on each other and tensions were now beginning to rise, and things were getting very nasty. Joe was a very stubborn man, but he was a firm believer in God and a regular church attendee. Every Sunday evening, Joe and his children would walk to and from church for the Holy Hour.

On one particular evening, the other farmers in the village, tired with Joe's stubbornness, decided to take matters into their own hands. As Joe approached the crossroads, which was a popular meeting place for the local men to converse on a Sunday evening, he saw a crowd of about twenty men gathered there. Some of them were holding clubs in their hands. Joe felt that he was in grave danger and prayed very hard to God to protect him and his children, from what appeared to be a lynch mob. Joe took hold of his children's hands and walked on, right through the men, who lined either side of the road. Joe glanced up and saw that the men had their heads bowed and were looking to the ground. Joe and his young family made it safely to the church, and on their return journey home, they found the crossroads clear.

Some years later, when the dispute was resolved, Joe called into the local public house for his weekly bottle of Guinness. Two local farmers approached him, and confessed to him that they had been planning on attacking him that Sunday evening all those years ago. Joe asked them why they had changed their minds. One of the men told him that they had decided against the attack because there had been at least fifty strong men surrounding him and his children, as they walked past. Joe had been unaware of his Angelic company that evening.

This story is a good example of the strength of Archangel Michael and how close by he is at all times.

Charlie's Angel Story: The Little Twin Boy

Back in 1992, the wife of one my close friends was undergoing chemotherapy treatment for cancer. Unfortunately, she became very ill. On the morning of her passing, my friend rang me and asked me if I would call to their home.

I went into the bedroom to see his wife, who was very ill. Their children, two daughters and two sons, were gathered around the bed. The doctor came around 10 am. At this point I went downstairs to make some breakfast for the family. I was still downstairs when my friend shouted to me to come up and say the Rosary. We knew that this lady was slipping away. Just as she was drawing her last breath, a little boy of about five years old appeared before me. Everyone else in the room seemed oblivious to his presence. I thought it was one of the grandchildren. I didn't think it was appropriate for a child to be in the room at this time, so I took his hand and lead him downstairs. I told him to watch television, but he just looked back at me with a very strange expression. I rejoined the family and we continued our prayers.

Later in the day, when we had returned downstairs, I noticed that the little boy was gone. I then asked the man who I thought was the child's father, where his son had gone, but he couldn't understand what I meant. A short time later, when this man's wife and children arrived, I realised that his son was much older than the child I had lead from the room, but they were very alike. That evening, at the wake, I told the family about the child I had seen in the room. They couldn't understand what I meant. I thought it was best to leave it. After all, they were still coming to terms with the loss of a loved one.

A few weeks later, whilst browsing through an old photo album, my friend showed me a picture of a young boy. It was obvious it had been taken a long time ago. Immediately, I recognised the child in the picture. It was the little boy I had seen in the bedroom that morning. My friend explained that the child in the photo was his wife's twin brother. He had passed over when he was only five years old.

The little boy had come to take his twin sister back home to heaven.

Fiona's Angel Story: My Guardian Angel, The Taxi Driver

One night, I got my handbag stolen when I was out in Belfast at a nightclub. I was looking for it, and my friends had left me in the club. It was the end of the night and everyone was being asked to leave as it was closing time. I was standing crying, outside the nightclub, as I had no money to get a taxi home to Glengormley. As I was standing there, a car pulled up and the driver said he was a taxi from a popular depot (back then taxis didn't display their name on the roof of the car). The man said to me:

"Get in and I'll take you out the road". I refused but the taxi driver replied: "Well, you can stand there if you like, but there is a crowd of fellas coming around the corner. Get in and I'll run you home." I got into the backseat of the car. I put the window down and held onto the handle, just in case I needed to make a run for it.

As we drove out towards my house, I experienced a feeling of calm and ease. The driver made me feel relaxed as we talked about work. When we got to my house I told him I would get my mum to pay him. He refused, but I insisted. My Mum also thanked him for bringing me home safely and asked him how much the fare was. He refused to take any money. After he left, my mum remarked: "What a nice gentleman that was."

The next day my mum phoned the depot to thank the driver once again, and to let his manager know of his good deed, but no one matching the man's description worked there. Mum phoned every depot in Belfast and Newtownabbey, but the driver could not be traced.

I can only assume he was my Guardian Angel, because, at no point, did he ask me where I lived; he just drove straight to my address.

Another great experience I had, when I was young, was seeing Padre Pio. I was going upstairs to my bedroom, when something at the top of the stairs caught my eye - a monk! He was standing on the landing, at the top of the stairs. He startled me and I ran into the living room to tell my mum. She said I had seen Padre Pio, and from that day on, I have been miraculously saved from quite a few near disastrous incidents.

I have started to have dreams, which have later come true. I can also see and hear spiritual beings on a regular basis. In the beginning, I was frightened, but now I take it all in my stride. It is comforting to know that I am not the only person who experiences these phenomena.

Lisa's Angel Story: A Visit In The Night

I usually sleep with eye pads on, to keep out the light, which streams through our bedroom window, because my partner prefers to keep the curtains open. One night, before I dropped off to sleep, a blinding light penetrated my vision. I assumed it was a car which had parked outside our gate, but then I realised, it was quite late for anyone to call. When this light kept shining, I removed the eye pads, and, to say I was startled by what was in our bedroom, is an understatement. The beauty which I beheld was incredible!

Beyond this extremely white light, Angelic faces appeared. In total, there were four beautiful Angels in the midst of this dazzling light. A great calmness descended upon me. As I turned to my partner, I saw another Angelic figure bending over him. As I studied each face before me, I recognised my Guardian Angel. He smiled and assured me that all was well. He told me the names of two of his Angelic friends, Marc and Diana. Diana had long, blonde hair; Marc's colouring was darker. I lay there ,staring at them for a long time; then things changed. On both sides of each of these Angels there were amazing coloured orbs. They kept swirling around them, reflecting and enhancing their beauty.

My partner was oblivious to what was happening around us. I felt privileged to have been visited by these heavenly beings. Eventually, I fell asleep and when I woke in the morning, they were gone.

Margaret's Angel story: A Protector In The Night

I had just passed my driving test, and I was very excited about taking my new second-hand car out for a spin. I collected my friend, who lived in a neighbouring town. As we drove around, I felt very proud of myself. After a while, I let my friend into the driving seat. With a lot of stops and starts, she drove for a short distance before we returned to her house, where we passed the time away, talking, laughing and playing music. Time went by very quickly and, before I knew it, it was very late. I hurried away, and as I was driving home, I realised I had left my purse and mobile phone behind. I wasn't worried. I knew I would get them the next day, so I continued my journey home.

As I was approaching a small roundabout, my car spluttered to a halt. I began to panic, as it was very late and there was no one around. I tried to start the car several times but it wouldn't start. I had no idea what to do! My only solution was to try and push the car into the side of the road and start walking the eight miles home. I was very scared, as I thought my parents would be very cross with me. I got out of the car, and as I did, I started praying very hard. It was then that I spotted three men coming along the street and my thought was that they would help me. Very soon, it became clear to me that they had quite a lot of alcohol taken and, somehow, I knew I was in danger.

I prayed and prayed and tried to start the car again, but with no luck. Then something happened that I will never forget! The telegraph pole across the street appeared to change into a giant of a man! I knew this person wasn't of this Earth. I just stood there staring at him! He was dressed in white and had long, black hair. My attention was then drawn back to the three men, when I heard one of them say: "Where did she go and where is the car that was parked on the roundabout?." Whether they got frightened, I don't know, but as best they could, they made off.

I couldn't believe it, as they walked right past me! It was obvious they couldn't see me. I looked back towards this being, who I now know was Archangel Michael, who had come to save me from imminent danger. I watched him slowly fade away until there was nothing left but the lamp post. I hurried back to the car and, as I turned the key, my car started instantly. I was so relieved! As I made my way home, I thanked this heavenly life saver, who I believe, came to my aid. I never forgot my phone or purse again!

Patrick's Striking Dream Visitation

A dear friend of mine has had many dream visitations, after the sudden passing of his beloved wife. One night, in one of his dreams, he dreamt he was in a hospital ward with his wife. The hospital was a very high building and his beloved wife was in a private ward at the top of this building. His wife lay in the hospital bed and was just about to give birth to their baby. Patrick was very concerned about the suffering of his wife and got up to look out of the large, bay window. Before his eyes, he saw an amazing water spout which was breathtakingly beautiful. His wife was in a lot of pain and said to him: "I think I am going to scream." To distract her, he went over to her bed and began to strum on the bed post, as the vision before them at the window was appearing to be growing larger. He then gently took her face in his hands and turned her towards the window so that she could see this magnificent sight. The brilliant water spout was full of dazzling, white light, and then it began to explode upwards and outwards. It was a truly magnificent display!

Suddenly, the white light from the spout changed into a striking stone church with glorious colours beaming from the windows. The vision in his dream kept alternating between the brilliant, white light and the stone church. This appeared to go on for a very long time. Then, two men were emerging from it and were walking towards them. In his dream, Patrick knew one was God, but he was unable to identify the second man. God and this other gentleman appeared to be walking closer to them. God was reaching out a golden book to them, but somehow Patrick was unable to grasp it. Though they were both mesmerised by this wonderful vision of God, and all before them, Patrick could see that his wife needed his attention, and possibly medical assistance, as her labour pains appeared to be getting very intense. In his dream he tried to call for medical help but, just at this point, Patrick woke up from his visionary dream.

Pondering, as to the meaning of Patrick's dream, a possible explanation could be linked to the fact that, in the early years of their marriage, Patrick and his wife suffered the loss of a baby. As each year passed, they often talked about how he would have looked and what age he would be, things that all grieving parents are likely to do. The dream appears to be a message to Patrick that his wife and son are now reunited in their heavenly home with God and that she is now taking care of their son. Patrick said he took great consolation from this dream.

Grace's Visit From The Angel Of Peace

Shortly after Grace's mother's passing, she had a visit from the Angel of Peace. She was grieving very deeply, owing to the sudden death of her mother, and she found the days following her mother's passing very painful. During this time, she had many visions of Angels and her mother appearing to her. Sometimes, she wondered if what she was seeing was in her imagination or if they were real visions. Grace's children were very young, and out of nowhere, they claimed they had seen Angels and their grandmother.

One particular Sunday evening, Grace was alone in her home and decided to go to bed for a rest. Understandably, she was emotionally exhausted and felt very low. As she lay on the bed, a very severe storm started, and with it came hailstones and severe winds. The hailstones were very large and they beat very loudly upon the roof. The noise was startling and it sounded as if the roof was going to cave in. Fear gripped her heart, as the thundering hailstones fell upon the roof, giving the impression it would collapse.

She began to pray, and all of a sudden, the room was full of Angels. The door to the bedroom was open and coming towards her, down the hallway, was a brilliant white orb. She prayed more and then the Angel of Peace was standing, in all her glory, at the doorway of the bedroom. The Angel stood with her hands outstretched, in a loving gesture towards her. Then, a great calmness descended upon Grace and she was no longer afraid of being on her own in the storm.

There was also a second vision of a young girl standing in the doorway, dressed in clothes from the 1800's. Lifting her phone to take a photograph of this vision, she wondered if the phone camera would capture it. However, later, she got the photograph developed and is now in the possession of an image of this wonderful vision. Very clearly, in this photograph, there were many Angel children, who seemed to be dancing above her wardrobe and standing in the doorway. The young girl stood with her head slightly bent.

One explanation of this vision is that the Angels are always around us, even if we cannot see them and that they will always be there for us in our time of greatest need, like the Angel of Peace was for Grace.

Jenny's Special Gift

Jenny, a close friend of mine, told me a remarkable story about a little girl who appeared to her when she was a student living in Belfast.

Her student accommodation was an old town house. When she returned home from college one evening, there standing in the hallway was a little girl, dressed in, what she can only describe as old-time clothing. Jenny said that the little girl looked happy and peaceful. No words were exchanged between the pair. After a short time, the little girl vanished.

Obviously, Jenny has the gift of seeing those who have passed on, particularly young people and children. I was fortunate enough to be present on another occasion when a young child appeared to Jenny. One afternoon, Jenny paid a visit to my home. Sitting down to have a catch-up with Jenny, she asked me who the child was that had entered the house and sat down beside me. She told me that the child had a strong resemblance to me. At this point, I told Jenny that I had lost a child, quite early on in pregnancy, many years ago. While I didn't see the child for myself, I have taken much comfort from what Jenny told me.

Dealing with a loss at anytime is never easy, particularly the loss of one so young, but it is reassuring to know that no matter how long it has been, those little children are still very much present, and a very big part of our lives, watching over us, as we continue to make our way on our life journey. Then, when we are called home to God, we will be reunited once again.

The Story Of An Angel Traveller

It was one morning in the month of May. My friend, Angela, called me and asked me if I could watch her children for a few hours, whilst she and her husband, Kenny, went to a funeral. I agreed. On arriving at their home, Nicole, Kevan and Eve were looking out the bedroom window. When I entered their home, Eve said to me: "Gwen, where is that wee boy who got out of your car with you?" and Kevan asked: "Who is he? Has he come to play with us?" Then, Nicole asked me if he was one of my grandchildren. I had come on my own, so I was certainly very interested in what they had seen. They kept on asking: "Where is he? Is he hiding? We want to play with him." Kenny and Angela looked at me, but I didn't reply. I assured the children there was no little boy travelling in my car with me.

Later on, when Angela and Kenny returned and we were all sitting at the table eating lunch, I asked the children about the little boy, but, as they were very young at that time, they were unable to describe him. The only information we could get from them was that he was pre–school, had black hair, and was wearing a blue jumper and dark trousers. Questioning them further, we drew a blank as to the boy's identity. They just kept repeating the initial story. Children can only tell us what exactly they see, so we had no choice but to believe them.

We concluded that I have a protective, travelling Angel, who the children were privileged to see.

Lucy's Angel Story

Lucy told me an amazing Angel story three years ago. It was winter time, and Lucy and her family had to travel quite some distance to pay their respects upon the sudden passing of a close, young relative. Setting off on the journey, Lucy was concerned about the dreadful road conditions, and about being unsure of finding the way. She decided to call on God and the Angels for protection on the journey.

They were travelling deep in the countryside, when, suddenly, out of nowhere, there appeared an emerald-green building. It appeared to be a restaurant named, 'The Green Angel.' Immediately, Lucy's spirits lifted. She now knew, and trusted, that the Angels would ensure that they had a safe journey.

When they arrived at the home of the deceased relative, there were a vast number of people in the house. On entering, Lucy and her family were amazed at the large number of beautiful butterflies fluttering around the coffin. It was really spectacular!

When they returned, a few days later, to attend the funeral, Lucy noticed that, during the burial, once again, there were hundreds of butterflies fluttering above the grave, as the coffin was being lowered. When the prayers were finished the butterflies disappeared.

We can conclude from Lucy's fascinating story, that the Angels, symbolised by the butterflies, were there comforting the grieving relatives and friends, with the reassurance that their loved one, was being looked after by God and his Holy Angels in our heavenly home.

My (Gwen's) Reassurances From My Loved Ones, From Heaven.

I was always delighted with all my divine encounters, but I was especially happy with visits from my husband and son, after they passed over.

One morning, shortly after Francis passed over, I was awakened by two hands resting warmly on my cheeks. Opening my eyes, I saw my husband bending over me. He was very happy and looked much younger than when he had left Planet Earth. I said: "Oh, Francis!" and in that moment, he was gone. I was greatly comforted, knowing that our loved ones are never far away.

Again, very shortly after my son, Kevin's, passing, I was in the den. On that particular evening, I was feeling very sad at the great loss of my son. Suddenly, the footrest of the reclining-chair, where he always sat, elevated into Kevin's usual resting position, and I just knew it was a message from Kevin, reassuring me that he is safely at home with his daddy. I felt a wave of love and comfort wash over me and I was filled with a wonderful sense of peace.

I have been privileged with many such visitations from my loved ones, who are now safely at home with God and I cherish every single one of them.

14
ANGEL MEDITATIONS (1)

In my life time, I discovered the prayer of meditation to be an uplifting way to spend time alone with God and the Angels. It is, for all of us, a very personal journey and one we make alone, which makes it special for us. It does not exclude the daily prayers we have always used; in fact it is a great enhancement of all prayer.

I will share with you some affirmations and meditations, which were sent to me. I hope they will help you find peace on your spiritual journey with God and your Angels.

Morning Meditation:

Say to yourself the following affirmation:

'I am happy, I am healthy and I am content.'

A new day has dawned and I would like you to think to yourself that this is your first day on Earth. How would you like to feel on your first day on Earth? - Woeful? Angry? Sad? Resentful?

No, as this new day has dawned, you want to be happy, joyful, peaceful, loving and content.

It is now time to thank God for this new day and to tell him that you will endeavour to make your first day on Earth uplifting and enlightening.

Day Time Meditation

As the morning passes, and the daily challenges of life are presented to me, I now call upon God and the Angels.

I ask Prince Michael to give me courage, strength and confidence to face all obstacles, which have arisen today or perhaps, may arise before the end of the day.

Night Time Meditation

As I lay myself down to sleep, I thank God and the Angels for my day, which has been filled with all my experiences, including happiness, love and joy.
Now, I ask my friend Archangel Raphael to bring me peaceful sleep, where my Guardian Angel will watch over me throughout the night and ensure that I get a restful night's sleep.

A Meditation To A Very Special Life-Long Friend

Begin by sitting down and breathing gently with your eyes closed. When you are totally relaxed, visualise yourself strolling down a lush, emerald-green, grassy field. You stand for a few moments admiring the spacious dimension all around you. Its simplicity of nature warms your heart and a sense of freedom envelopes you.

As you walk, you notice the abundance of many wild flowers, how they flourish and blossom without any help, except from Mother Nature. Now you see a formation of golden rock situated alongside a small, fast-flowing stream. With arms outstretched, you race down the hill towards this stream, enjoying the warm, gentle breeze flowing through you. You're feeling a sense of freedom, as you leave all your worries and cares behind you.

Finally, you arrive. You are quite surprised when

you discover the rock has seats hewn out of it. The middle seat has your name clearly written on it. You sit down on this special seat. Holding your head upwards towards the sun, which is just coming out from behind a silver cloud, you know it has come out for you.

You become aware of the many birds singing sweetly all around you. As you look into the clear, crystal water of the fast-flowing stream, you watch the formation of ripples quickly passing by. You ponder these ripples as to what they mean to you. You follow them downstream as they disappear around a corner. You come to understand they are a sign to you, of the past. And you know the past is gone forever. Looking upwards, to your right, you are unable to see the true formation of the ripples that are coming towards you. Now, it dawns on you the meaning of this. It is a sign of the future, whic for now, is a mystery. This discovery helps you to realise how futile it is to worry about the past or the future.

You sit there, peacefully, for a long, long time.

In the stillness of this wondrous dimension, you listen to the strains of magical heavenly music starting to play. You somehow know this music is heralding the entrance of someone special.

Your attention is now drawn to a very bright, white light approaching you. Out of the mist of this light, a beautiful, young Angel walks towards you and sits down beside you. The Angel greets you warmly, calling you by your first name and then assures you of how much you are loved by God and the heavenly world. You ask the Angel: "How do you know me?" The Angel replies: "I have known you forever. I am your very best friend, your Guardian Angel. God has delegated me to walk every step of the way with you, on your Earthly journey."

Your Angel now tells you: "When you need help, ask me and if it's for your higher Spiritual well-being, it will be done. If God knows what you ask for will damage you, it will not happen. A caring mother does not give a nice, shiny razor blade to her baby, even though the baby cries out for it. She knows the baby will harm itself with it. Instead, she brings other, safer toys to the baby, just as God gives us safer gifts. You and your Angel talk at great length, about your life and your hopes and dreams for you and your family.

Now, it is time for you to leave this beautiful, sacred sanctuary of yours. You tell your friend you must return to Earth and your Angel smiles and says: "I am going too." You feel very excited at finding this wonderful new friend. As you stroll back up this plane, you ask your Angel: "What is your name?" Your Angel smiles and tells you his/her name. You now can greet your Angel by name. You feel very secure, knowing you are never alone as you journey through life. You give thanks to God for sending you this special friend.

It is time now to take a few deep breaths and, once again, feel yourself sitting on your chair.

Protective Meditation Seeking The Help Of Our Great Archangel Michael

Find a place and time, where you will not be disturbed for approximately fifteen minutes. Close your eyes and breathe gently. Visualise yourself walking down a beautiful, golden, sandy beach. You feel the heat of the sand, as you walk in your bare feet and an amazing energy streams through your body, bringing you a sense of warmth and contentment. A gentle breeze carries you down to the water's edge and, as you watch the golden sun rise far out over the ocean, you know this is your new dawn of peace and tranquility. You stand in the refreshing ripples of water, sinking your feet down into the sand. Feeling the water washing over your feet and ankles, you become aware of how all negative thoughts are dispersing, bringing you to a place of Godly love. You stand there for a very long time, not particularly thinking of anything. Then, in the distance, and in the stillness of the morning, you hear a gentle roll of drums.

Looking around, your attention is captured by a breathtaking, deep-blue mist which has appeared close to you on the beach. Slowly and quietly the mist descends upon you. Out of the mist emerges the most beautiful Archangel you could ever have imagined. This great warrior strides towards you, calling you by your first name and announcing to you: "I am the great Prince Michael, your protector and guardian." The golden crown he wears is studded with priceless gems, glistening in the bright sunshine, as does his golden sapphire-handled sword. He speaks to you now in a soft, loving voice: "Come, little Earth child, let's walk the great beach of life together."

He takes your hand and, at this moment, you feel a sense of freedom from all your worldly concerns and cares. Prince Michael invites you to tell him how you are coping with Earth life and, before you know, you are telling him about all your worries and concerns, perhaps disappointments, rejections, hurts and the times when you have suffered from feelings of justified anger and resentment. And all the while you are telling him about these human errors, not once do you feel judgements are being made of you. Archangel Michael now speaks to you with loving, reassuring words: "God's little Earth child, have no fear, we are watching over you. In times of stress, remember to use the gifts God bestowed upon you, when your divine soul joined your body."

He now takes off the golden crown he is wearing and begins to place in your heart, one by one, the gift of Godly Power, Love, Patience, Forgiveness, Holistic Assertiveness, Courage and Acceptance of yourself and all others. Now you know you have recovered these gifts and that you will use them to fulfil your hopes, dreams and goals, which will carry you through life's journey.

You thank Archangel Michael for visiting you,

and he reminds you that he stands on your right hand side, in the wings of your life, helping you to feel safe and protected, at all times. He says to you: "Breathe my name and I am there."

It is time, now, for you to leave your beach and return to Earth life. As you stroll away from the beach, listening to the echo of Michael's voice assuring you of God's love and his protection, you know this journey with Archangel Michael will stay with you forever.

An Enlightening Meditation To Archangel Raphael

Sit down in a relaxed position and allow your mind to enter a timeless zone. In the silence which envelopes you, gently inhale and exhale, breathing out all worldly thoughts from your mind. You now find yourself standing on the top of a hill. As you look down, far below, you marvel at the simplicity of your dimension, as you stare at the lush, emerald-green grass which covers a vast area beyond you. You see a figure standing very tall, and you hear a voice softly calling you. You race down the hill and, lo and behold, you encounter this magnificent, heavenly being! With a welcoming smile and tender words, he invites you to join him. You marvel at the love and beauty of his Angelic countenance.

He tells you: "I am the great Archangel Raphael.

God has delegated me to bring comfort and healing to the people of Earth. Come, my child, let us sit together and you can tell me in which area of your life you need God's healing."

You now feel very relaxed, as you sit under the blazing sun, in Raphael's emerald-green valley. You feel the healing and love energy from this wondrous Angel. You speak to him at great length, about your life, and the areas in which you feel you need guidance. Then, there is silence for a few moments, before he speaks comforting words to you. He tells you he is your life-path guide, and that there are times when the path presents obstacles on your journey through life. However, it is in overcoming these obstacles that you learn to cope with Earth life. In turn, this helps you to understand God's great plan for you, to reach your full potential spiritually.

He also says that during these trying times, you are never alone: "I am by your side." He then gives you a plan to follow: "Dear Earth child, when you look after your emotional and mental bodies, your physical and soul energy will reap the rewards of this exercise and you will enjoy good health. The simple way to nurse your two etheric bodies is practising self love, and acceptance of who you are, and know that God only creates the most perfect."

He also invites you, in so as far as you can, to avoid negative situations, and to remember you are not always totally to blame when conflict arises in any area of your life. He now clears away all negativity from your etheric bodies and you feel refreshed and complete, in the love of God. It is now time for you to thank Archangel Raphael and he reminds you he is never far away: "Call my name and I am there."

You stroll back up the hill and, on reaching the top, you look back and marvel at the wondrous beauty. You know you will return to this amazing dimension one day, sitting under the sun-drenched beauty of life itself.

It is now time to return to your daily Earth life, with the knowledge that you are fully supported by God and his army of Angel workers.

As you return to your daily life, you sit down for a few moments and ponder over the wise words of Archangel Raphael, who is the Angel of love, peace and harmony. You reflect upon what he told you about the accumulation of negative energy on your etheric bodies and aura. You now realise the importance of cleansing, so that the seven beautiful colours of the aura are bright and clear, thus bringing you to a place of peace and harmony.

When we are in a state of peace and harmony with ourselves, we are in a state of peace and harmony with the whole universe.

15
THE TRIANGLE OF LIFE

One morning, the following images appeared on my bedroom wall:

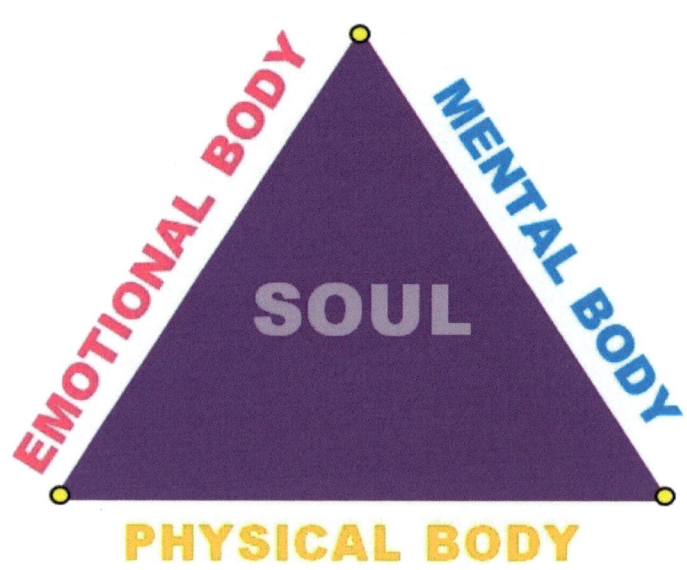

It took me some time to understand the meaning of the message that the Angels were sending me. As I studied this triangle, with its radiant colours of yellow, pink, blue and purple, it slowly dawned on me, that the colours represented the realms of our entire bodies. The pink is our Emotional Body, the blue, our Mental Body, and the yellow our Physical Body. In the centre, is our Soul, the largest part. The previous image, shows our complete bodies, together, when in peace, balance and harmony.

The image, below, represents the occasions when there is an imbalance between our four bodies: the Mental Body, the Physical Body, the Emotional Body and the Soul. You can clearly see how the sides have become detached from the Soul.

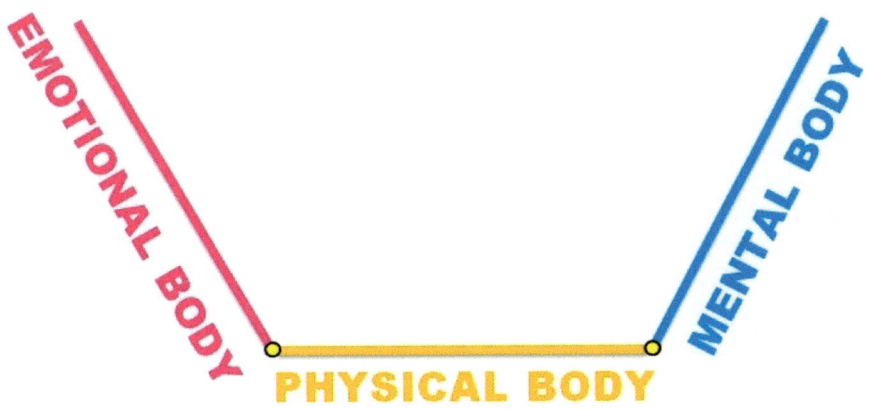

16
ANGEL MEDITATIONS (2)

Helpful Meditation to Archangel Gabriel:

Imagine sitting down in your favourite armchair under a beautiful, old oak tree, drinking in the warm sunshine and feeling a gentle breeze pouring over your whole body. You look around and marvel at the deep-blue sky above, and you feel energised by the nature and wonder of God's creation of the planet you dwell on. Gently, you breathe in this invigorating greatness of nature.

After a while, totally relaxed, you amble down this country lane, and your attention is now drawn to nature, as you smell the various aromas surrounding you. You pause to smell the wild honeysuckle, the freshly mown grass and, as you look over the low cut hedges, you feel compelled to travel further down this lane. Walking in your bare feet, you feel the softness of the emerald-green grass, giving you comfort. You wonder why there is no one else around and then you realise this is one of your sacred and secret sanctuaries. You feel very excited and wonder what's in store for you today.

On and on you stroll, and then you come to a corner and, as you do, you see this beautiful picturesque, white gate and how it is adorned with the most breathtaking, colourful roses, cascading wildly, down onto your path. Approaching the gate and opening it, you enter into a wondrous dimension, full of colour, and filled with the strains of soft, Angelic, Godly music. As you stand there, in wonder, at the sight before you, your thoughts are: "Is this my eternal home?" Your Guardian Angel is now at your side, smiling, and he/she invites you to come further into your very own paradise garden. Just for a moment, you believe you have been here before. You spot a finely-chiselled chair in gold, which you decide to sit in to admire the beauty before you. You observe the many nature Angels who tend to your garden, how busy they are, and you listen to the choirs of Angels and how sweetly they sing God's praises. You notice many birds in this garden; they seem to be joining in with God's heavenly, Angelic choir. Many exotic butterflies are floating around and, at times, you believe this is part of your welcome home. Time passes, and now you become aware of a mighty Archangel approaching you, calling out your name. As you rise to greet him, he announces: "I am Archangel Gabriel, God's messenger, and I have come to help you." He reassures you of how God loves you and wants you to be happy. He reminds you of the importance of expressing how you feel, in a loving, creative way and says: "If you do, joy will fill your heart, thus avoiding any depressing thoughts. Life on Earth can be made very stressful for you and stress is the biggest killer of man kind." He adds: "Do not get caught up in the rat race. Be your own person, and remember, as an adult, you, and only you, are in charge of your life."

He now invites you to walk through this picturesque garden, through the many colourful flowers and green leafy trees. As you do, you pass many flowing waterfalls and fountains which are filled with clear, crystal water. This great Archangel invites you to drink of this healing water. Archangel Gabriel is God's messenger and he has a message for you, which is sent to you from God. He says: "Take my hand and come with me." On the way, you meet many nature Angels. Then, this wonderful Angel leads you to a spectacular, white building, which is God's great art gallery. As you and Gabriel enter in through a magnificent, golden door, you're amazed as you scan through the many books on display. He smiles and tells you: "There's a special book here which is yours!" He then encourages you to choose your book from the shelf. You look around for sometime, and at last you find it, noticing how your name is carved across the front of it, in gold. Now, he invites you to open the book at a certain page where there is something special written. It's God's special message, and at this moment, when you read it, you know it's the answer to your prayers.

It is time now, for you to leave your paradise garden. You thank Archangel Gabriel for making your visit to him such a memorable one. As you leave, he reminds you: "Remember, we are waiting for your call and we will be there."

You now return to Earth life and you know, as you continue on with your mission, you will never be alone. God invites you to be joyful and contented and to do the best you can.

As you leave, you hear the choirs of Angels singing your praises. Slowly, you walk down that lane, pondering on what you have seen and heard today.

Meditation To Archangel Uriel

On awakening from life's slumber and hypnotic state, you find you're sitting in a small, grassy garden adorned with many wild flowers: buttercups, daisies, violets and many more. In the distance, you admire the purple hues of colour, radiating from the sun-kissed mountain. As you start breathing in the warm rays of colour blowing gently towards you, you feel a sensation of love and peace. You are very happy and content in this cosy, little garden of yours, as you listen to the song of the blackbird. Quite some time has passed, before you become aware that you are surrounded by a leafy, high hedge which surrounds your special sanctuary. You now notice an opening in the hedge. Arising, you decide to explore.

Approaching the opening and peeping beyond, you're startled by the beautiful rain-spattered woodland, and you know you have discovered another secret hideaway. You thank God for the many, wonderful, special opportunities he gives you to spend time alone, to commune with your heavenly friends.

Following the rugged path in your new-found woodland, you stop to enjoy the beauty of the wildness around you. You take time to watch, as the birds build their nests, squirrels gather nuts and wild rabbits scurry along. All of this brings back happy, childhood memories of picnics in the woods and joyous times gone by. Ascending a hill towards the peak of this rapturous place, you come to a standstill. Looking ahead, you see the outline of a very tall, heavenly Archangel, and it seems as though everything has been enveloped in holy silence. The only sound you hear is the soft music and sweet voices of Angels humming and crooning.

This heavenly being calls out to you to join him, and your heart leaps with excitement. He opens his arms and welcomes you home. His loving words of acceptance and love comfort you as he wraps his cloak of purple and gold energy, with sparkles of white, around you. Like all God's Angels, no words can describe the beauty which emanates from him. He tells you: "I am the Angel of Peace and Prayer, and I have come to assist you, as you journey through life, in reaching your full potential spiritually."

All forms of prayer are pleasing to God. Archangel Uriel encourages you, not only to talk to God, but to listen, and in your Holy silence your soul will cry out in joy at the splendour of heaven's peace.

Sitting with this quiet, gentle energy alongside Uriel, you enjoy the sound of the babbling brook you are sitting at, and you feel the healing energy pouring over you; it's as if you have arrived safely home. After a long, comfortable silence, Archangel Uriel quietly speaks to you. He says: "Let nothing disturb you. All is in divine timing and everything is as it is meant to be. Do not fill up the suitcase of life with regrets and past human errors. Only remember the happy memories. As you rise to greet each new day, decide that, no matter what your day may bring, you will make at least one good memory. In the future, when you look back, on your life, you will find you have more good memories than negative memories."

You know it's time for you to leave and go back to Earth to continue with your great mission, which God has delegated to you.

Sadly, you say goodbye to Uriel, but you come away with a wealth of knowledge and wisdom. As you look back to wave to your friend, you know you will return again to sit in the company of love, freedom and silent prayer.

Archangel Michael's Cleansing Meditation

Sit quietly and begin by breathing in a purifying, blue-coloured energy. Now, visualise the etheric sheath above your head. Then, imagine your aura, which is made up of seven shining colours. Above this is your etheric tube. Your etheric tube begins at you left ankle at birth. As you grow and age, it grows with you. It is a beautiful, brilliant, white light, likened to that of The Holy Spirit energy. In early childhood, there is no debris within the tube, but, as life goes on, due to hurtful and painful experiences, our etheric tube becomes blocked.

Archangel Michael tells us the importance of keeping this tube clear. When we reach our middle to late fifties, our etheric tube can burst, if not cleared from time to time. Then, it can spill out its poisonous energy throughout our body. It is at this point that our physical body begins to suffer from aches and pains, which cannot be accounted for by medical science. When conflict arises, between ourselves and others and, for some reason or other, we cannot address it, we become angry and resentful.

With eyes closed, we can scan our etheric tube, checking to see if there are any dark patches or bulges in it. If so, we now call on the Great Prince Michael to clear it for us. As he clears it for us, we watch the dark energy fall from this tube. Slowly our tube returns back to its beautiful, healthy state. It is now time to say thank you to Archangel Michael, and to God, for this wonderful friend he has given us.

Archangel Michael Cord-Cutting Meditation

Cords are formed when conflict arises between ourselves and certain negative situations, and the negative actions of others towards us. For some reason, or another, we are unable to come to terms with these situations at the time.

Visualise yourself walking through one of your special sanctuaries. You know that you are on your way through this enchanting mountain pass to meet some very special friends. Your attention is now drawn to the heralding of Angelic voices singing God's praises, as you prepare to meet with Archangel Michael and Archangel Chamuel. You look up and see these two amazing figures, walking towards you, waving and smiling. They invite you to walk with them. You feel very relaxed as the cool breeze gently caresses your face. They congratulate you on how you are fulfilling God's Earthly mission.

Happily, the three of you walk across the scenic mountain-top. Archangel Michael takes you by the hand and leads you into this beautiful, quaint building called "Ye olde-world cottage." You stand in awe as you gaze at the golden thatch upon its roof and the welcoming, golden half-door opened for you and your friends. On entering the cottage, you see a magnificent gold, marble bed. Michael invites you to lie down on the bed and to look down at your two sides, to check if there are any unhealthy cords growing there. Cords on your left-side will denote an emotional trauma. Cords on your right side represent a hurt you have suffered from an outside influence, for example, in the neighbourhood or workplace.

You now ask the powerful Archangel Michael to help you to detach from these cords. He hands you his golden sword. As you place your hands upon the blue, sapphire handle, you feel the gentle touch of Michael's hands enclosing yours. On the count of three, you slash through these cords simultaneously.

Now, quietly say to yourself: "I now release myself, and you, of all known and all unknown negative karma. The God in me salutes the God in you. Thank you."

Glancing back at your sides, you notice the cords are now gone. You feel a wonderful sense of freedom. You watch as Archangel Chamuel, surrounded by his wonderful, pink energy, leads away any persons or situations with which you may have been in conflict, and you know you have sent them away in God's love.

You leave this picturesque cottage, with a feeling of love, peace and contentment. You thank these two great Archangels for their divine intervention. It is now time to return to your Earth life, knowing that, in the future, you will always know, if necessary, you can return at any time and cut any negative cords you may have grown.

A Beautiful Meditation To The Risen Jesus

Wandering through a wonderful, colourful valley, you look up at the deep-blue sky, noticing the amazing rays of gold emanating from the warm sun. You start breathing long, deep breaths from these rays, and you feel a deep sense of peace and tranquility, as you exhale all worldly thoughts from your mind. Joining you now, is an old friend of yours, your Guardian Angel. As always, when you meet, you both have much to talk about.

Your Angel now invites you to take another path and, before you know, you have now entered a beautiful desert. You feel the warm, golden sand between your toes. It almost feels like a Godly beauty, far beyond human imagination. You, and your Angel find a large, golden rock, where you sit down. Looking around this sanctuary of yours, you observe how sparse everything seems, but in this sparseness there is a quiet beauty that brings a glow to your soul. Now, you see a small dot in the distance. As you watch this dot coming towards you, you are intrigued as to how it seems to grow into a familiar figure. You get very excited, as you realise it is the Risen Jesus. As He nears, you rise to greet him. Then you hear Jesus call your name and his love and acceptance of you overwhelms you. Your very soul cries out with joy! Jesus sits down beside you and, taking your hand in friendship, he smiles and says: "Welcome, my Earth Child, to our heavenly home. Come now, let us converse and pray together." Bowing your head, you talk to Jesus about your life on Earth, your hopes and dreams. You ask Him for advice, as to how you can successfully accomplish your great mission, which God has delegated to you. Now, it is time to remain in silence, as you listen to Jesus speak to you. After a long time, you know it is time to say goodbye to Jesus for now. As you both stand up and Jesus lays his healing hands upon you, you feel elated, and thank Him for coming to you. He reminds you, as always, that He is always here for you.

Now he is gone. You watch him as he strides across the desert, and you know you can return to this special, secret place to meet Jesus at any time. It is now time for you and your Angel to leave this desert and return to Earth life. You thank your Angel for leading you to this special sanctuary, where you have met the Golden One.

The Lord's Prayer:

Our Father who art in heaven
Hallowed be thy name
Thy kingdom come
Thy will be done on earth as it is in heaven.
Give us this day our daily bread
And forgive us our trespasses
As we forgive those who trespass against us
And lead us not into temptation
But deliver us from evil
Amen.

Lord Jesus, please surround
My home with your Golden Energy
and bless everyone
Who enters into it.
Standing in prayerful silence,
We now receive a Golden
Blessing from Jesus.
Amen.

ANGEL INSPIRATIONS BY GRAINNE KEOGH-KELLY:

Hope and prayer soar up high,
Building bridges in the sky.

A Prayer sent to God on the wings of an Angel.

When peace and calm are within,
The sea of life will greatly ripple.

Love is the key to unlocking all your troubles and woes.

Embrace the beauty of colour,
Savour the smell of the roses.

Look deep within,
The surface is but a speck of your greater self.

Sleep tonight, and forever,
In the arms of an Angel.

PRAYERS FOR PROTECTION

I now encircle myself, Lord Jesus,
With your Godly light of healing.
Please bless me, guide me
And protect me from all
Harsh karma, now and always,
Amen. Thank you.

*

Lord Jesus, envelope me in your Golden Light.
Archangel Michael, envelope me in your Courage.
Archangel Raphael, envelope me in your Love and Healing.
Archangel Gabriel, envelope me in your Joy and Happiness.
Archangel Uriel, envelope me in your Holy Silence,
So I can sit in the presence of God Amen.

17
ARCHANGEL MICHAEL'S CLEARING EXERCISE (to remove negative energy)

In 2005, I became more spiritually aware of the effects of negative energy that are present in our world, and how this negative energy affects our auras. When negative energy seeps into our bodies, we can be left feeling emotionally and physically drained. Knowing that Archangel Michael is the Angel of Positivity, I prayed to him, asking him for guidance. A few days later, he appeared to me and showed me this Clearing Exercise.

Feet apart and hands outstretched.

Sweep your hands over the back – hands slightly apart.

Take your two hands over the left side of the head and sweep down the body, past the heart, down the left leg and drop. (Drop the negative energy onto the floor. Do not touch the floor.)

Sweep over to the right foot and bring your hands up the right side of your body.

Rest your left hand on your heart.

Turn your right hand around into a cupping position. Push the energy up as far as you can over your aura. Sweep your outstretched, right arm over your head and bring down to almost meet the left hand, but not touching.

Sweep your two hands down the left leg and drop the negative energy onto the floor.

Place your hands behind your two ankles.

Sweep your hands up the back of your legs and curl your hands up your back, as far as you can – keep your hands apart and push the energy up.

Bring your hands to the front of your body and

sweep them over the front of your shoulders and catch the energy, using a grasping action.

Then sweep your hands over the left side of your head and sweep down the left hand side of your body, down past the heart and drop the negative energy onto the floor.

Straighten up. Sweep right hand over the left hand, wrist, elbow, shoulder and up the left hand side of your head, across your chest, heart and down the left hand side of your body. Drop the negative energy onto the floor.

Straighten up. Sweep your left hand over your right hand, wrist, elbow, shoulder and up over your head and go down the left hand side of your body, past your heart and drop the energy onto the floor.

Bend over and sweep all the negative energy you have dropped onto the floor, into your cupped hands. Lift the negative energy into your cupped hand and stand up.

Put the negative energy into the fire, or a bowl of water. Alternatively, throw the negative energy down the toilet bowl, flush quickly and close the toilet lid.

Archangel Michael's Exercise To Envelope Your Body In Positive Energy:

The negative energy is now gone from your body. To envelope your body with positive energy, the actions are reversed. As we started at the top of the body with clearing the negative energy, we now start at the right foot, to surround our bodies with positive energy.

Feet apart.

Place your two hands on your right foot, touching the clean floor and bring your hands up your right leg. Rest your left hand on your heart.

Turn your right hand around into a cupping position and with your outstretched arm, sweep right through the aura to meet the left hand.

Sweep your hands down the front of your left leg to the floor and seal in the positive energy by touching the floor.

Sweep your hands up the back of your two legs and cup your hands up your back as far as you can.

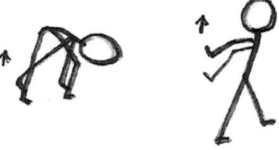

Bring your hands to the front of your body and sweep them over the front of your shoulders and catch the positive energy, using a grasping action.

Sweep your hands over the left side of your head, past your heart and down the left hand side of your body to your left foot. Seal in the positive energy by touching the floor.

Straighten up. Sweep your right hand over your left hand, wrist, elbow, shoulders, head and over your face and down your left leg and seal in the positive energy by touching the floor.

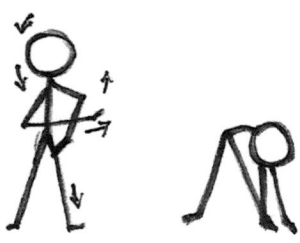

Straighten up. Sweep your left hand over your right hand, wrist, elbow, shoulders, head and over your face and then bring your two hands down your left hand side, past your heart and down your left leg and seal by touching the floor.

Straighten up. Close your eyes; outstretch your arms slightly with fingers closed.

Bring your hands quite close together.

Move your arms and hands out and in slightly, until it feels like there is an elastic band between them. When you get this feeling, gradually widen the space between your two hands, while continuing to move your hands in and out. This helps you to feel your own positive energy.

ABOUT THE AUTHOR

Gwen was born of Irish-German descent on 30th December 1942 in Belfast, to her parents, Charlotte and George Wolfe. She was the only living daughter of a family of six.

Gwen spent most of her childhood in Hillsborough. While Gwen faced many challenges at this young age of her life, she has many fond memories of happy days of playing around Hillsborough Castle, fishing on Hillsborough Lake and visiting her kind neighbours and friends. When she was twelve years old, she moved with her family to Draperstown, a small market town at the foothills of the Sperrin Mountains, in County Derry. When Gwen first arrived in Draperstown, she knew this was her true home.

Childhood for Gwen, was a very confusing time. She knew that she had a special gift - not everyone could see and speak to Angels. At the age of fifteen, she met Francis McAuley and it wasn't long before the pair became great friends. Even in her youth, Gwen very quickly realised that he was the love of her life and that one day they would marry.She was right.

On the 8th January 1963, what was to be one of the happiest days of her life, she married her soulmate, Francis. Together, Francis and Gwen were blessed with five healthy sons, Peter, Kevin, Stephen, Conrad and Philip.

Throughout life, Gwen has continued to see spiritual beings and Angels. There were also many times when she experienced premonitions and dreams about world disasters. Gwen also has had visions of Our Lady, Padre Pio and deceased loved ones.

Raising her boys was the busiest time in Gwen's life. Not only did she oversee the running of the household, but she also helped to manage the family's bakery business.

Life was not straightforward. There were many trials which Gwen and her husband had to face together. One of their biggest challenges was her husband's diagnosis with cancer in 1989. It was after her husband's diagnosis that Gwen called on the Angels for support. Afterwards, she began to see these heavenly beings more often. These visits from the Angels were, and continue to be, a source of great comfort to her.

Today, Gwen no longer conceals this special gift that she has been given. Instead, she regularly meets with other like-minded people to share and discuss all their experiences.

By opening up and sharing these precious moments, Gwen has been able to help others, who like her, have been confused by out-of-this-world experiences. Now, with Gwen's guidance, they can acknowledge that the ability to see beyond the physical dimension, is a true gift from God.

My Life On Earth With The Angels

Gwen Charletta McAuley

Printed in Great Britain
by Amazon